The Provoked Economy

Do things such as performance indicators, valuation formulas, consumer tests, stock prices or financial contracts represent an external reality? Or do they rather constitute, in a performative fashion, what they refer to?

The Provoked Economy tackles this question from a pragmatist angle, considering economic reality as a ceaselessly provoked reality. It takes the reader through a series of diverse empirical sites – from public administrations to stock exchanges, from investment banks to marketing facilities and business schools – in order to explore what can be seen from such a demanding standpoint. It demonstrates that descriptions of economic objects do actually produce economic objects and that the simulacrum of an economic act is indeed a form of realization. It also shows that provoking economic reality means facing practical tests in which what ought to be economic or not is subject to elaboration and controversy.

This book opens paths for empirical investigation in the social sciences, but also for the philosophical renewal of the critique of economic reality. It will be useful for students and scholars in social theory, sociology, anthropology, philosophy and economics.

Fabian Muniesa is a researcher at the Centre de Sociologie de l'Innovation, École des Mines de Paris. He looks at calculation, valuation and organization from a pragmatist standpoint, with a focus on the problems of business pedagogy, managerial performance, financial innovation and economic reasoning.

Culture, Economy and the Social
A new series from CRESC – the ESRC Centre for Research on Socio-cultural Change

Editors

Professor Tony Bennett, Social and Cultural Theory, University of Western Sydney; Professor Penny Harvey, Anthropology, Manchester University; Professor Kevin Hetherington, Geography, Open University

Editorial Advisory Board

Andrew Barry, University of Oxford; Michel Callon, École des Mines de Paris; Dipesh Chakrabarty, University of Chicago; Mike Crang, University of Durham; Tim Dant, Lancaster University; Jean-Louis Fabiani, Ecoles de Hautes Etudes en Sciences Sociales; Antoine Hennion, École des Mines de Paris; Eric Hirsch, Brunel University; John Law, The Open University; Randy Martin, New York University; Timothy Mitchell, Columbia University; Rolland Munro, Keele University; Andrew Pickering, University of Exeter; Mary Poovey, New York University; Hugh Willmott, University of Cardiff; Sharon Zukin, Brooklyn College City University New York/Graduate School, City University of New York

The *Culture, Economy and the Social* series is committed to innovative contemporary, comparative and historical work on the relations between social, cultural and economic change. It publishes empirically based research that is theoretically informed, that critically examines the ways in which social, cultural and economic change is framed and made visible, and that is attentive to perspectives that tend to be ignored or side-lined by grand theorizing or epochal accounts of social change. The series addresses the diverse manifestations of contemporary capitalism, and considers the various ways in which the 'social', 'the cultural' and 'the economic' are apprehended as tangible sites of value and practice. It is explicitly comparative, publishing books that work across disciplinary perspectives, cross-culturally, or across different historical periods.

The series is actively engaged in the analysis of the different theoretical traditions that have contributed to the development of the 'cultural turn' with a view to clarifying where these approaches converge and where they diverge on a particular issue. It is equally concerned to explore the new critical agendas emerging from current critiques of the cultural turn: those associated with the descriptive turn for example. Our commitment to interdisciplinarity thus aims at enriching theoretical and methodological discussion, building awareness of the common ground that has emerged in the past decade, and thinking through what is at stake in those approaches that resist integration to a common analytical model.

Series titles include:

The Media and Social Theory (2008)
Edited by David Hesmondhalgh and Jason Toynbee

Culture, Class, Distinction (2009)
Tony Bennett, Mike Savage, Elizabeth Bortolaia Silva, Alan Warde, Modesto Gayo-Cal and David Wright

Material Powers (2010)
Edited by Tony Bennett and Patrick Joyce

The Social after Gabriel Tarde
Debates and Assessments **(2010)**
Edited by Matei Candea

Cultural Analysis and Bourdieu's Legacy (2010)
Edited by Elizabeth Silva and Alan Ward

Milk, Modernity and the Making of the Human (2010)
Richie Nimmo

Creative Labour
Media Work in Three Cultural Industries **(2010)**
Edited by David Hesmondhalgh and Sarah Baker

Migrating Music (2011)
Edited by Jason Toynbee and Byron Dueck

Sport and the Transformation of Modern Europe
States, Media and Markets 1950–2010 **(2011)**
Edited by Alan Tomlinson, Christopher Young and Richard Holt

Inventive Methods
The Happening of the Social **(2012)**
Edited by Celia Lury and Nina Wakeford

Understanding Sport
A Socio-Cultural Analysis **(2012)**
John Horne, Alan Tomlinson, Garry Whannel and Kath Woodward

Shanghai Expo
An International Forum on the Future of Cities **(2012)**
Edited by Tim Winter

Diasporas and Diplomacy
Cosmopolitan Contact Zones at the BBC World Service **(1932–2012)**
Edited by Marie Gillespie and Alban Webb

Making Culture, Changing Society (2013)
Tony Bennett

Interdisciplinarity
Reconfigurations of the Social and Natural Sciences (2013)
Edited by Andrew Barry and Georgina Born

Objects and Materials
A Routledge Companion (2014)
Edited by Penny Harvey, Eleanor Conlin Casella, Gillian Evans, Hannah Knox, Christine McLean, Elizabeth B. Silva, Nicholas Thoburn and Kath Woodward

Accumulation
The Material Politics of Plastic (2014)
Edited by Gay Hawkins, Jennifer Gabrys and Mike Michael

Theorizing Cultural Work
Labour, Continuity and Change in the Cultural and Creative Industries (2013)
Edited by Mark Banks, Rosalind Gill and Stephanie Taylor

Comedy and Distinction
The Cultural Currency of a 'Good' Sense of Humour (2014)
Sam Friedman

The Provoked Economy
Economic Reality and the Performative Turn (2014)
Fabian Muniesa

Rio de Janeiro
Urban Life through the Eyes of the City (forthcoming)
Beatriz Jaguaribe

Devising Consumption
Cultural Economies of Insurance, Credit and Spending (forthcoming)
Liz Mcfall

Unbecoming Things
Mutable Objects and the Politics of Waste (forthcoming)
By Nicky Gregson and Mike Crang

Centre for Research on Socio-Cultural Change

The Provoked Economy
Economic reality and the performative turn

Fabian Muniesa

LONDON AND NEW YORK

First published 2014
by Routledge
2 Park Square, Milton Park, Abingdon, Oxon OX14 4RN

and by Routledge
711 Third Avenue, New York, NY 10017

Routledge is an imprint of the Taylor & Francis Group, an informa business

© 2014 Fabian Muniesa

The right of Fabian Muniesa to be identified as author of this work has been asserted by him in accordance with sections 77 and 78 of the Copyright, Designs and Patents Act 1988.

All rights reserved. No part of this book may be reprinted or reproduced or utilized in any form or by any electronic, mechanical, or other means, now known or hereafter invented, including photocopying and recording, or in any information storage or retrieval system, without permission in writing from the publishers.

Trademark notice: Product or corporate names may be trademarks or registered trademarks, and are used only for identification and explanation without intent to infringe.

British Library Cataloguing in Publication Data
A catalogue record for this book is available from the British Library

Library of Congress Cataloging-in-Publication Data
Muniesa, Fabian
The provoked economy : economic reality and the performative
turn / Fabian Muniesa.
pages cm. – (Culture, economy and the social)
Includes bibliographical references and index.
1. Economic indicators. 2. Economics–Statistical methods. 3. Finance.
4. Value. I. Title.
HB137.M86 2014
306.3'6–dc23
2013044024

ISBN: 978-0-415-85713-0 (hbk)
ISBN: 978-0-203-79895-9 (ebk)

Typeset in Times New Roman
by Cenveo Publisher Services

Contents

Acknowledgements   ix

Introduction   1

PART I
The problem of performativity   5

1 A few theoretical rudiments   7

The performative turn in the social sciences 7
Four distinctive philosophical problems 17

2 The consideration of economic reality   28

Studies in the constitution of economic things 28
Economic naturalism against the practice
  of economizing 35

PART II
Elementary case studies   43

3 Recounting financial objects   45

The investment bank as a puzzle 45
The back office and the trouble with finalization 48
Processing descriptions through the banking space 50
Singular objects and written confirmations 52
The valuation of financial objects as a problem
  of description 55
Technocratic mastery and back office intricacy 58

4 Discovering stock prices — 61

Making market perfection algorithmically explicit 62
Potential, real, virtual and actual prices 69
The trouble with second-order transparency 72
Provoking prices of particular kinds 75

5 Testing consumer preferences — 79

Performativity and the marketing simulacrum 79
Taming the test, taming the market 82
Becoming a measuring instrument 86
The experience of elicitation as provocation 88
The sociology of market testing 91

6 Realizing business value — 96

The hermeneutics of the business subject 97
The object of valuation and the intuition of capitalization 103

7 Indicating economic action — 108

Masses of performance targets and indicators 109
Political or economic action 113
Quantifying scientific production 118
Indicating an economic effect 121
Provoking a state of economy 123

Tentative conclusion — 127

Bibliography — 131
Index — 158

Acknowledgements

Most of the ideas on which I elaborate in this book emerged during conversations with friends and colleagues. I would like to thank: Catherine Grandclément, Javier Lezaun, Signe Vikkelsø, Dominique Linhardt, Emmanuel Didier, Antoine Hennion, Horacio Ortiz, Liliana Doganova, Álvaro Pina-Stranger, Marc Lenglet, Niki Panourgias, Alaric Bourgoin, Véra Ehrenstein, Başak Saraç-Lesavre, Anne-Sophie Trébuchet-Breitwiller, Alexandre Mallard, Guillaume Yon, David Pontille, Martin Giraudeau, Claes-Fredrik Helgesson, David Stark, Barbara Czarniawska, Donald MacKenzie, Yuval Millo, Daniel Beunza, Talha Syed, Giuseppe Mastruzzo, Andrew Barry, Paul du Gay, Isabelle Stengers, Philippe Descola, Patricia Falguières, Anders Blok, Andreas Mayer, Annie Cot, John Law, Evelyn Ruppert, Celia Lury, Noortje Marres, Ellen Hertz, Marion Fourcade, Bruno Latour and Michel Callon. To these last two, Michel Callon and Bruno Latour, I owe the kernel. I hope they accept that I dedicate this book to them.

The book is based on the essay that I submitted in 2011 to fulfil the requirements of my Habilitation à Diriger des Recherches (HDR) degree at the Université Paris-Dauphine. I thank Isabelle Huault for her guidance and support, and the members of the assessment committee, Philippe Lorino, Paolo Quattrone, Ève Chiapello, Hélène Rainelli and Hervé Dumez, for their thoughtful critique.

This work has been supported by a Starting Grant of the European Research Council (Grant Agreement 263529, April 2011 to March 2015). I thank the public administrations and research communities that cooperated in the assessment and implementation of this project. Acknowledgments are due to my home institution, the École des Mines de Paris, and in particular to the Centre de Sociologie de l'Innovation, the crucible of my speculative self. Part of this writing benefited from visits to a number of institutions. I thank the International University College of x *Acknowledgements*

Turin (June 2011, February 2012), Columbia University (August 2011), and Harvard Business School (April 2012) for their hospitality and stimulation.

The original empirical materials that illustrate the book's main points come from a number of past investigations. Chapter 3 borrows from an earlier research project carried out at the London School of Economics in collaboration with Susan V. Scott, Marceline Ducrocq-Grondin and Dominique Chabert (Moving Markets Research Project, January 2003 to December 2003). Chapter 4 is inspired by materials elaborated in the context of a doctoral research project funded by France Télécom R&D (January 1999 to December 2002). Chapter 5 is based on a collaborative empirical investigation with Anne-Sophie Trébuchet-Breitwiller (July 2007). Chapter 6 draws from exploratory work to prepare and develop parts of the project funded by the above-mentioned ERC Starting Grant (February 2010 to December 2012). Chapter 7 revisits an enquiry conducted in collaboration with Dominique Linhardt as part of a research project funded by the Agence Nationale de la Recherche (Grant ANR-05-BLAN-0391, January 2006 to December 2008).

I would finally like to thank Penny Harvey, Kevin Hetherington and Tony Bennett, editors of the CRESC Series at Routledge, for their trust and support, and Kara Stephenson Gehman for her help with my English.

Introduction

Consider, for example, a consultancy slideshow. A management consultant shows a diagram to her clients depicting their firm's problems. The diagram points to potential solutions that the consultant is ready to demonstrate. But, you know how consultancy works. Last week (perhaps also last night) the slideshow was still an erratic draft. The consultant was concerned with the diagram's layout, the visuals, the keywords, the smack of seriousness, the montage. At some point she was whispering to herself, 'theatre, theatre'. Today, she is committed. She whispers to herself, 'communication, communication'. Overall, the slideshow works well. True, some clients whisper the same words to themselves. But they see the firm's problems, realize their implications and recognize new ideas for strategic solutions. The presentation turns felicitous. Was it not a montage, though?

Consider now a valuation formula. A financial analyst is busy crunching data in order to obtain some reliable figures about the value of an asset that her employer, a private equity fund, is likely to acquire. Some mathematics is involved. The formula indicates the rate the targeted company is expected to pay to its creditors or its owners. The formula is a convention, and hardly anybody expects it to be absolutely accurate. The analyst knows that, but she uses it mainly because everybody else does, and also because she needs to use something and the formula is there, available. She also knows, as you do, that the data may be flawed, that the company's value is ultimately uncertain and that she is basically tinkering. Yet, the figures are calculated, and a financial decision is solidly based on them. On tinkering?

Consider, finally, a consumer test. A decision needs to be made about the launch of a new product, and the marketing department is commissioning some market research for the brand. A market researcher is analysing the results of a series of tests in order to discern consumer preferences. You have seen how such tests are done: people are selected randomly, exposed to the product and asked to complete a questionnaire; sometimes they also are asked to express personal opinions in a group discussion (the proverbial focus group). The market researcher is quite used to the routine. She is familiar with the artificial nature of the process. Does she ever express preferences like that when she finds herself strolling around in the supermarket? Not quite. But here comes the marketing report: a picture of consumer preferences, a picture of the real market. Or is it?

All three examples (and many others you could come up with) share a common problem. These three artefacts (the consultancy slideshow, the valuation formula, the consumer test) pose the question of the reality they represent. They also pose the question of the reality they effect. And those two questions, although not exactly the same, are complicatedly entwined. What do these artefacts refer to? Is that reference really real? And if not, what is it? Is it a sort of lie? Is it a game? Nonetheless, are the effects produced by these artefacts real? What kind of reality is that, though? All of these questions refer to a problem that I call the problem of performativity. This book is an attempt to solve this problem, or at least to contribute to a judicious understanding of it.

How does this book do that? What you will find here is mainly a reflection of a theoretical nature tested through a series of empirical investigations. The reflection is grounded on a pragmatist understanding of signification as process and of reality as effect. Such an understanding can be detected in a number of contributions to the interpretation of economic things, sometimes clearly articulated, sometimes not. I briefly review them, with a view to spotting common concerns. But the reflection can also be informed by some novel conceptual developments. I contribute by elaborating a number of concepts that my empirical research has obliged me to engage with, namely: description, simulacrum, explicitness and provocation. The empirical accounts presented here are not (and could not be) straightforward applications of such concepts. They stand rather as tests that generate novel angles for reflection and comprehension. Their function is to be inspirational. And this function does not anticipate any straightforward disciplinary obedience, either from the reader (for you are just an enquirer dealing with problems that are comparable to the ones I came across), or from the writer (for I am definitely not a regular sociologist, nor am I a professional philosopher, observing anthropologist, or conventional organization scientist).

In Part I, I discuss the problem of performativity in economic reality. The first chapter is devoted to a discussion of the intellectual roots of the idea of performativity in the social sciences and in philosophy. The particular blend of pragmatism I ascribe to is contextualized and explicated. It is in this chapter that I introduce the analytical vocabulary that I use in the rest of the book. In the second chapter, I discuss performativity in relation to economic reality, with a short literature review. The reader is provided with a few indications of where this work stands in relation to the broader landscapes that must be taken into account in tackling the 'provoked economy'. I also provide a theorization of what can be expected to happen when something is referred to as being economic (e.g. economic reality).

In Part II, I use a series of empirical studies to flesh out the perspective. These are: an examination of the back office in an investment bank (Chapter 3), a historical study on stock exchange automation (Chapter 4), an ethnography of consumer testing (Chapter 5), a commentary on the pedagogy of financial valuation (Chapter 6) and an analysis of public management reform in France (Chapter 7). The chapters are based on original research but are not in-depth renderings of empirical investigation. Rather, they represent, as strongly as possible, the intellectual contributions that can be extracted from that research relative to the question that I set out to examine here. Their aim is to foster intellectual imagination and to provide suggestions for further enquiry, rather than to be seen as closed investigations.

Part I
The problem of performativity

1 A few theoretical rudiments

The idea of performativity has two facets. One, now quite widely discussed in the social sciences, is rather clear and perhaps even a bit banal in some respects. It refers to operational knowledge, reflexive modernization, performative utterances, the effects of science, the theatricality of practice, and so on. All are quite different, but in my opinion they do share some features in the understanding of performativity. The other facet, perhaps less understood, is more profound in its philosophical engagement. It links to pragmatism and comparable currents of thought, as well as to classical discussions on the reality of ideas. One crucial point here is that reality is really real when it is provoked (and, hence, realized). However, let us start with the first facet.

The performative turn in the social sciences

The expression 'performative turn in the social sciences' is perhaps a bit misleading. First, the notion of performativity (or the idea of the performative) has been used in a variety of ways which are often unrelated and perhaps even contradictory, in reference to speech, theatre, efficacy, and so forth. There is, as far as I can say, no integrative, consensual, coherent view on this and we are therefore in the somewhat uncomfortable, but quite fertile ground of ambiguity. Second, identifying an intellectual turn requires situating a relevant shift in a particular time and place, which is unlikely in cases such as the one to be examined here. It is a well-known fact that novelty in the social sciences is almost systematically accompanied by the rediscovery of old precursors. So the performative turn that I am examining here is not a clear-cut epochal shift, nor a complete intellectual revolution, nor a coherent, self-conscious endorsement of a unique doctrine. Yes, it

8 *The problem of performativity*

may actually resemble a U-turn in some respects. But, it is a turn resulting from reflexive movement, a change in direction. Allow me to explore aspects of such a turn and discover the path it may take.

Performativity in postmodern knowledge

To my knowledge, one of the first authors to have used the term 'performativity' (*performativité* in French) in relation to social-scientific matters was Jean-François Lyotard in his 1979 report on 'the problems of knowledge in most highly developed industrial societies' (Lyotard 1979a). The report was commissioned by the Department of Higher Education (Conseil des Universités) of the provincial government of Québec, and then famously published as a book with a quite resounding title: *The Postmodern Condition* (Lyotard 1979b, 1984). The report's topics of interest included, most centrally, a focus on how the production and use of knowledge in advanced industrialized societies affect the characteristics of knowledge proper. In particular, Lyotard noted, the materialization of knowledge as an object of production and use (and, in some respects, of productivity and usefulness) provokes an emphasis on practicality and technicality which translates into a crisis in the legitimacy of grand narratives. Knowledge about things no longer occupies an overarching, critical, general and properly modern position but is now, in a sense, part of the industrial functioning of things. Postmodern knowledge is performative knowledge.

But what does 'performativity' exactly mean in this context? Lyotard dealt with a variety of facets of performativity. He referred to the pragmatics of language, performative utterances, speech acts, language games and authors such as John L. Austin and John Searle. He also mobilized, quite appropriately, work in the semiotics of science and technology and its implications for the study of society. The notion of 'actor–network theory' did not yet exist at that time, but its premonition was visibly at work in the footnotes (e.g. Michel Callon was quoted in Lyotard 1979a: 103, 1979b: 34–5, 1984: 90–1). That said, Lyotard did use the notion of performativity only in the restrictive, particular sense of a performance drive. Performativity, he indicated, characterizes an industrial logic of optimization – or, more prosaically, the rules of achievement in business – and, by extension, the dominant criteria for the legitimization of scientific research and higher education in a postmodern environment (Lyotard 1979a: 16–17, 24, 59–75, 1979b: 25, 34, 69–88, 1984: 11, 17, 41–53). Lyotard himself tried to reconcile, rather rapidly and clumsily in my opinion, the terminology of performative utterances and the idea of performativity in the sense of technical efficiency, saying that 'Austin's performative realizes the optimal performance' (Lyotard 1979a: 98–9, 1979b: 21, 1984: 88). I do not quite understand the meaning of this obscure assertion, but I think that the fact that it mixes up the concept of the performative utterance and the economic ideal of optimization is revealing.

From my perspective, Lyotard's report captured some relevant traits of what I call here the performative turn. Performativity is indeed, in part, about performance in the purest sense of efficacy in the achievement of tasks and operations. It is true that effectuation (i.e. the act of effecting, of bringing about) is, in general terms, a distinctive aspect of this interpretation of performativity that is shared with other instances of the performative turn in the pragmatics of language, the dramaturgical understanding of action or the anthropology of science. We are, in a sense, looking in a vaguely similar direction. But this distinctive aspect of the performative turn also has its own relevance, in particular to the social studies of business, management, industry and labour.

The sociology of human work and of industrial organization has often pointed toward the machine as both an operational metaphor and an organizational instrument. Pierre Naville's work on the sociology of industrial automation was perhaps pivotal in that direction, at least in France, together with more contemporary elaborations of the sociology of labour techniques (e.g. Benjamin Coriat's and François Vatin's) that all highlighted, in one way or another, the practical consequences of the performance drive that governs the technologies of industrial organization (Naville 1963; Coriat 1979; Vatin 1987). The engineer-led French literature on 'managerial instruments' also exacerbated performance in the face of systematic views of the organization (Lorino 1989; Moisdon 1997; Segrestin 2004; Lorino and Teulier 2005; for a genealogy and a sociological assessment see Aggeri and Labatut 2010; Chiapello and Gilbert 2013).

Luc Boltanski and Ève Chiapello's *New Spirit of Capitalism*, a landmark in the sociological critique of business, is perhaps one of the key investigations that focused on the growth and transformation of the vocabulary of performance in contemporary capitalism (Boltanski and Chiapello 1999, 2006; see also Jany-Catrice 2012; Du Gay and Morgan 2013). Management critiques of various styles have also emphasized the consequences of a culture of industrial fluidity, task efficiency and performance measurement, with performance measurement at the centre of a burgeoning critical literature in accounting and management studies (e.g. Knights and Willmott 1999; Townley *et al.* 2003; Chapman 2005; Alvesson *et al.* 2009). These and comparable streams of literature share what could be labelled a critique of the operational that meets, to a large extent, the concerns identified by Lyotard. As postmodern knowledge deploys its performative purpose (mostly in the form of managerial techniques), authors speaking from critical positions are burdened with the uncomfortable task of commenting on performativity as either a critical impediment or a critical opportunity (Fournier and Grey 2000; Spicer *et al.* 2009).

The performative idiom in the sciences

Performativity is also best known to some as something distinctively associated with the ideas of Michel Callon. Commentators in this area usually refer to Callon's foundational introduction to a collection of essays titled *The Laws of the Markets* (Callon 1998; see also Callon and Latour 1997; Callon 1999). The so-called 'performativity programme', which seems to have originated there, is indeed often considered to be a speciality in economic sociology or in the anthropology of markets (see Fourcade 2007). However, the idea comes, as Callon himself does, from science and technology studies, an area in which performativity is, first and foremost, about the institutive capacities of scientific or technical knowledge and about the types of realities that are brought into existence or modified throughout scientific ventures. It is, in a sense, quite remarkable that one of the first groundbreaking studies to have followed Michel Callon's scheme in the analysis of markets was conducted by Donald MacKenzie, who is also a reputable sociologist of science and technology (MacKenzie 2001, 2003, 2004, 2006, 2007).

Andrew Pickering provided quite a cogent and useful clarification of the understanding of performativity in science studies (Pickering 1995). He played what he called a 'performative idiom' against a 'representational idiom' in the understanding of science: the latter 'casts science as, above all, an activity that seeks to represent nature, to produce knowledge that maps, mirrors, or corresponds to how the world really is' (Pickering 1995: 5). This way of understanding science, he added, 'precipitates a characteristic set of fears about the adequacy of scientific representation that constitute the familiar philosophical problematics of realism and objectivity' (Pickering 1995: 5). A number of researchers in science studies would agree and find this statement to be quite at odds with what actually happens in scientific activity. What happens, for example, is that objects turn objective because they are provoked (literally, created) in the laboratory. What happens is that observations are nothing but chains of mediation that require the mutual configuration of the observed world and the observing apparatus. What happens is that models do actually work as machines (that is, they perform like machines), even when they are abstract models, in which case what counts is the verb – the act of abstracting; the model abstracts; it is an abstractive machine. What happens is that the boundaries between science and technology are more than fuzzy when one actually looks at science in action.

Taking all of this into account (or at least a decent part of it) is entirely about siding with the 'performative idiom' in the study of science, and that move is very recognizable in quite a large number of what are now widely acknowledged contributions (e.g. Hacking 1983; Latour 1987; Galison 1997; Cartwright 1999; Mol 2002; Daston and Galison 2007; see also Jensen 2004 for a lucid overview). Bruno Latour, in particular, has been struggling very actively to defend the rationale of this realist account of science, especially against commentators who would wrongly identify a penchant for the unreal in this 'performative idiom', more naturally termed 'constructivism' in scholarly discussions (Latour 1999). Yes, here constructivism becomes realism. For reality is indeed constructed, but it so in the engineer's sense: the scientific fact stands objectively in the laboratory as the bridge stands firmly over the water, that is, insofar as it undergoes a laborious process of material assemblage. But that is not, alas, quite a common view. For constructivism to mean realism it has first to emancipate from the idea of 'social construction' that is often found in the social sciences and according to which reality would be located not in things but in what we think of them. And for realism to mean constructivism it has to avoid the temptation of considering reality as something that just stands there, placidly, without taking the trouble to happen. The performative turn in science studies can be read as a contribution to this demanding rapprochement.

Expression as performance

But performativity is also about the idea of practice as ongoing accomplishment, as acting and staging in an almost explicitly theatrical sense – or at least one that considers the practical and situated features of sense-making in ordinary life. This meaning of performativity is particularly relevant to cultural studies and gender studies (e.g. Butler 1993; Bell 1999, 2007; Kosofsky Sedgwick 2003), but also to practice-based, interactionist perspectives in organization studies (e.g. Feldman 2003; Lounsbury and Crumley 2007; Gherardi and Strati 2012) and to the dramaturgical analysis of organizational practices and events (e.g. Mangham 1990; Clark 2008; Biehl-Missal 2011).

One guiding idea here is perhaps best formulated through Erving Goffman's now classical perspective: that of the 'theatrical performance' and the 'dramaturgical' principles hence derived for sociological enquiry into 'real life' (Goffman 1959: xi). The interplay between expression and impression that characterizes situations of presenting oneself are analysed in terms of performances, that is, activities which serve the purpose of creating an effect on others. With the performer being more or less cynical or sincere in relation to the authenticity of the part she is playing, and the setting being more or less appropriate to the felicity of the act, we end up quite naturally with the problem of the reality of the performance (Goffman 1959: 17–76). Goffman explicitly opposed a dichotomy between 'real performances' (i.e. 'something not purposefully put together, being an unintentional product of the individual's unselfconscious response to the facts in his situation') and 'contrived performances' (i.e. 'something painstakingly pasted together, one false item on another, since there is no reality to which the items of behaviour could be a direct response') and he basically said such a dichotomy amounts to 'poor analysis' (Goffman 1959: 70).

What are we left with, then? Goffman first pointed to the intricacies of reflexivity, not quite reducible to a sharp distinction between theatrical innocence and theatrical guilt. But, perhaps more importantly, he indicated that what counts as the 'solid world' in the performance is what is effected – and how well. Then, disappointingly enough, he went on to quote Jean-Paul Sartre's infamous conjecture on the waiter in a café who is supposed to be 'playing at being a waiter in a café' and who 'plays with his condition in order to *realize* it' (Goffman 1959: 76, for a sharp criticism see Bourdieu 1981). But the word is there, appropriately emphasized in the original (Goffman's and Sartre's): realize. What a pity that this notion was left somewhat unpacked by Goffman. Before the quotation, in a discussion on the performance of social status, Goffman had just written that the latter is 'something that must be enacted and portrayed, something that must be realized' (Goffman 1959: 75). And to realize something means both making sense of that thing and making that thing real, enacting it, doing it. Note that the same productive ambivalence is present in French: *réaliser*.

One can perhaps find in Harold Garfinkel's work a more refined formulation of the problem, without a focus on theatre or performance as such, but retaining an emphasis on social order as accomplishment, as an achievement of constitutive practice (Garfinkel 1967). There is a long record of interesting contributions along these lines in workplace studies (for example, see Rawls 2008). Enquiries into the production of subjectivity through the display of identity and indeed most of the vocabulary used to discuss enactment and performance in social-scientific parlance do also generally invoke, in my view, the performative turn we are briefly examining here (Bell 2007; Loxley 2007).

I want to conjecture here how this version of the performative turn is connected, perhaps in a most symptomatic manner, with the particular blend of intellectual culture that emerged in post-World War II North America, particularly in New York City and on college campuses in California. This includes, on the one hand, performance art, happenings and the dissolution of the fourth wall in theatre, with leading artists such as Julian Beck, Allan Kaprow, John Cage, Andy Warhol, William Burroughs and others; and, on the other hand, experimental methods in the social sciences, group therapy, psychodrama and other methodologies for the contained generation of social situations, mostly advocated by authors such as Jacob L. Moreno, Kurt Lewin, Stanley Milgram, Paul Lazarsfeld, Robert K. Merton and Wilhelm Reich, all of whom were concerned, in one way or another, with the development of a social-scientific, small-scale solution to the great European horror. The performative ethos of realization interlocked in that peculiar cultural environment was determinant in the transformation of the idea of how the social ought to be rendered in the social sciences (Lezaun *et al.* 2013).

Signs that organize

Different elaborations around the idea of the performative characterize different bodies of specialized research. The vocabulary of performativity also has been developed to quite an extent in semiotics and, more precisely, in the semiotics of organizations – or rather of organizing, as many practitioners of this speciality prefer to say, in order to emphasize the fact that organization, just like signification, is an action, a process. François Cooren has authored particularly cogent and handy accounts of the potentials of the semiotics of organizing, that nicely complement the work of James R. Taylor and Elisabeth J. Van Every, other prominent members of the 'Montréal School' (e.g. Cooren 2000, 2010; Taylor and Van Every 2000, 2010; Cooren *et al.* 2006). Cooren in particular pointed to the fact that the semiotic approach should not stop at the analysis of what is said about and within organizations. He worked out the link that exists between processes of signification and organizational agency, in a direction quite comparable to other notable contributors to the semiotic anthropology of writing and of the maintenance of writing (e.g. Denis and Pontille 2010a, 2010b, 2010c). This means observing how things become organized through texts, inscriptions and conversations, and how aggregate actors such as corporate organizations can grant themselves the capacity to act in their own names. In short, the semiotics of organizing is about analysing how things are accomplished with signs, which is plainly about performativity (Cooren 2004). Cooren conceived the semiotics of organizing, in part, as an extension of speech act theory, drawing explicitly from John L. Austin and John Searle.

This type of work connects quite notably with interpretive perspectives developed in organization studies by authors such as Karl Weick and Barbara Czarniawska (e.g. Weick 1995; Czarniawska 1997). The tradition known as symbolic interactionism (or sense-making perspective, after Weick's motto) often has been reported to be grounded in pragmatism, with reference to George Herbert Mead. That is, in fact, the version of the pragmatist legacy that is closer to the field of social psychology, sometimes also to behaviourism. Using that framework, a discussion about symbolic interactions would not refer to interactions between signs. Rather, such a discussion would focus on interactions between people through the use of signs, and how the formation of the individual mind depends on this process of sharing signs (or meanings). But there are many blends of pragmatism, and for some it would be entirely satisfactory to talk instead about interactions between signs, interpreted, if at all, by other signs (and not by an individual interpreter). That would be the case for Charles S. Peirce for instance, the inventor of pragmatism from my perspective. I refer the reader to the devastating critique of Charles W. Morris (credited for transforming Peirce's theory of signs into a window of opportunity for psychological interactionism) briefly put forward by John Dewey in defence of Peirce (Dewey 1946; for a vast clarification see also Kockelman 2013).

The semiotics of organizing presented by authors such as Cooren rather demonstrates a materialist understanding of semiotics, one that sides not only with Peirce, but also with the continental blend of semiotics developed by Algirdas Julien Greimas, and in particular with his actantial model. The notion of actant, which initially was proposed as a way to study the structure of agency (what acts, what causes action) in texts, was then adopted by authors such as Bruno Latour, Michel Callon, Madeleine Akrich and John Law for the development of a generalized theory of agency known as actor–network theory or the sociology of translation (see Dosse 1995, 1999 for a genealogy, and Law 1994 for the implications for organizational ethnography). Actor–network theory is an explicit reference in Cooren and in other notable contributions to the material semiotics of organizing (e.g. Czarniawska and Hernes 2005). The basic tenet of actor–network theory is as follows. If I write, for example, 'France embraces nuclear power', I then proceed to analyse how agency (i.e. the capacity and position to act, force others to act or be activated) is rendered in both the sentence and the wider text where it originates (say, from an unapologetic official account of nuclear power in France). But I do not stop at that, since I consider that this sentence is an empirical one and that it is embedded in a network of instituted documents that ultimately refer to France as embracing nuclear power. I therefore proceed to the empirical interpretation – the 'unscrewing' (Callon and Latour 1981) – of this actor called France, this act of embracing and this thing called nuclear power. In other words, I see how nuclear France holds together (is organized) or not as a compound assemblage of networks of designation – an actor–network (see Hecht 1998 for a source of inspiration). Perhaps I can even say that I see how nuclear France is performed, although the performative is so pervasive for actor–network theory and its correlates in the material semiotics of organizing that the word itself becomes superfluous most of the time.

A vaguely similar (pragmatist) direction

So the performative turn in the social sciences is, it seems, characterized by a variety of ideas which, for the purposes of this discussion, I have sorted into four groups. These are neither closed nor exhaustive, of course. Ideas in the first group emphasize technical performance in the achievement of tasks and operations, an emphasis that partakes of a distinctively postmodern type of applied, industrial, entrepreneurial, managerial and operational knowledge. Ideas in the second group focus on the institutive capacities of science, how scientific ventures provoke, set up, prepare or instantiate the realities under scrutiny in contrast with a view of science as depiction. Ideas in the third group relate to enactment, a theatrical understanding of the idea of representation, and the active play and display of meaning in the ordinary work of making sense of things, people and oneself. Ideas in the fourth group focus on the practical efficacy of signs, their action, and their articulation in enunciation apparatuses that serve the purpose of getting things organized and done, corresponding to a semiotic (and at the same time materialist) view of organized practice.

Do all of these ideas indicate the same movement? My answer is yes, to a large extent. What is common among all, implicitly at least, is an idea of signification as act (to signify is an active process) and of reality as effectuation (to effect is to bring reality about). What is also shared, concomitantly, is an intellectual background often referred to as pragmatism. That label, 'pragmatism', is perhaps as ambiguous as the notion of performativity. Occasionally, it has been used to refer (wrongly, in my view) to a somewhat floppy subjectivism with a behavioural tinge, sometimes augmented with some kind of mild existentialism, and at other times confined to a subspeciality of linguistics (i.e. performative utterances and the pragmatics of interlocution). To be clear, when I use the term pragmatism, I am referring to the intellectual tradition in philosophy that is known for emphasizing the two ideas (or the two aspects of the same idea) that I just summarized: reality as effectuation and signification as act. This intellectual tradition is often associated with the names of people such as Charles S. Peirce, William James and John Dewey, and, as a result, often linked to the shaping of North American liberal thought and to its contexts: the Progressive Era, the Great War, the Roaring Twenties and the rise of corporate America, the Wall Street Crash of 1929 and the Great Depression (Purcell 1973; Menand 2001; Lears 2009). But pragmatism is also recognizable, as I will show, in other contexts and other times.

Take the word πράγμα *(prâgma)*: a thing, a thing done, a fact. It is striking that early advocates of the term pragmatism (James 1907: 352, 2000: 25) mistakenly emphasized 'action' or 'practice' in the word's Ancient Greek etymology over 'fact'. This probably paved the way for attractive although basically mild understandings of pragmatism (c.f. Peirce 1905). This oversight, however, is somewhat useful. At least in my understanding of pragmatism, the emphasis is not on things just as things, but on things happening. A fact is an act: the act of taking place. At the core of this philosophical engine lies the idea, which was best expressed by Charles S. Peirce in his writings on the theory of signs, that signification is an action that takes place, which is why things signify things (Buchler 1955).

My summary of the pragmatist direction (reality as effectuation and signification as act) does not in fact summarize the pragmatist tradition, in the sense of the speciality of North American thought. It is just a direction, and as such it can sometimes (and sometimes not) be identified in the tradition of the same name. Likewise, pragmatism can sometimes (and sometimes not) be spotted in the studies that I have alluded to in this section and in the questions that I am about to pose in the next one, which is a slightly deeper (and closer to my own) philosophical exploration of the 'performative turn'.

Four distinctive philosophical problems

So, we now have an idea of reality as effectuation and of signification as act. But this is more than an idea. It is a philosophical problem. There is no way I can provide here (or elsewhere) a truly philosophical examination of the nature of the problem. But I can provide a few thoughts on the problem, or on four versions of the problem. These are intended to be instrumental in the rest of this essay and should serve this purpose insofar as they remain bound to empirical questions. The first is about description, about the kind of thing that a description produces. The second is about the simulacrum, about its truth and effects. The third is about provocation, about what it means to say that reality is really real when it is provoked, and hence realized. The fourth is about explicitness, about what it is for reality to accommodate explication. Unsurprisingly, all of these problems are related to the topics explored in the rest of the essay: markets, the economy, business and capitalism.

The problem of description

Discussions on performativity often struggle with the problem of description. The problem, more exactly, is in distinguishing between two types of situations. On the one hand you may have statements, methods, texts and other apparatuses that are meant to describe a reality that is exterior to them. That is, an external state of affairs is reported by recording or transcribing something, either in a very realistic manner, or in an approximate, stylized or perhaps even abstracted way. Regardless of whether such a report refers to an already existing thing or to something that does not really exist (i.e. a future project, a hypothesis, or just an idea), the thing that is described is supposed to be external to the description. The description is, of course, not the same as the described thing as there are transformations going on, but there is a thing indeed. And one can describe a fictitious thing, but a fictitious thing, as its name indicates, is a thing. On the other hand, you may have statements, methods, texts and other apparatuses that are meant, explicitly, not to be descriptions, but rather to instantiate or effect their own reference. These include proposals, instructions for an artefact, dramaturgical performances, institutional declarations, expressions of oneself, *mots d'ordres*, and so forth. One could argue that these, too, are descriptions. However, what they describe is not external to them (or at least not completely), and they fall, quite easily, into the realm of the performative.

I just wrote 'on the one hand' and then 'on the other hand', but it is clear from the writing that those two hands hold each other. The distinction corresponds in a way to the widely advertised linguistic division between so-called constative (or descriptive) and performative utterances, famously put forward by John L. Austin in the *William James Lectures* given at Harvard University in 1955 (Austin 1962). The division may very well hold together. But Austin himself seemed to object to its neatness. In my interpretation, he clearly pointed to the fact that as soon as something is stated (which thus constitutes the event of the statement), it becomes performative indeed, because to state something is an act (Austin 1962: 148–52). This problem, of course, has been widely discussed in the literature, especially in relation to the fact that being performative positions a statement (or any other type of referential apparatus) in a problematic situation vis-à-vis the truth of its reference (e.g. Récanati 1982; Loxley 2007). A rigorous, pragmatist-like understanding of truth as the effect of the active act of referencing is not always welcome. See, for instance, the terms of the struggle in Bruno Latour's constructivist case for scientific truth (Latour 1999) and its metaphysical assessment (Harman 2009), or John Law's defence of methodological soundness in the midst of performativity (Law 2004).

In fact, what counts in my view, at a more general level (that is, one that does not limit signification to the domain of linguistics and that enters deeper into a pragmatist, materialist philosophy of signification), is that descriptions add to the world. Descriptions may differ in their style of reference. Here, I am afraid that there are more than two categories, and I believe Austin would agree. But they are all facts, things that happen, events. They may refer to something that is already there but they definitely add to reality, too. They provoke a new situation, a new ontological deal: one in which there is a description.

Description (or writing, for that matter) supplements reality in the sense put forward by Jacques Derrida in his critique of Jean-Jacques Rousseau (Derrida 1967). That is definitely one thing to take into account.

As we will see, this is something to take into account in the anthropology of the economy. One type of economic object which is particularly suitable for this discussion is the financial derivative contract. This is a product, a financial product that can be bought and sold, that can be referred to in a variety of ways, a product that can be described from a variety of angles: price, terms, risks, etc. Describing these products can be tricky, especially in the case of complex products with multiple underlying clauses, pricing parameters, accounting and legal constraints, forecasting methods, and potential purposes. Investment banking is, in a sense, the name of an activity that essentially consists of describing these things. But what is under that pile of descriptions? What are these financial derivatives contracts anyway? Well, these are nothing more and nothing less than descriptions themselves. A financial derivative contract is a document that describes its conditional behaviour and the terms of payment. It is an act of writing compounded by the act of forwarding the written file to the market (which is itself another pile of descriptions). These are, for example, the terms in which Elie Ayache, philosopher and quantitative financier, clarified the nature of the derivative in a marvellous book, *The Blank Swan*, that explicitly considers finance as the realm of the performative and contradicts a probabilistic view of derivatives as referring to underlying states of the world (Ayache 2010). One of Ayache's favourite sources for the philosophical examination of all this is Gilles Deleuze, a philosopher whose theory of signification would be as close as one could get to the original pragmatists (e.g. Deleuze 1969: 22–35, 1990a: 12–22).

The way that you describe, define, write, depict or express a financial derivative product thus affects (or, more precisely, effects) the way it is traded and behaves. Recent, crucial contributions to the social studies of finance have implicitly or explicitly demonstrated this point on a variety of financial objects (e.g. Maurer 2002a, 2002b, 2005; MacKenzie 2003, 2006; Lépinay 2007a, 2007b; Millo 2007; Huault and Rainelli-Le Montagner 2009; Karl 2013). Because we are discussing description (and, therefore, performativity) as a philosophical problem, doubts emerge about the kind of reality that these financial objects possess. If there is some performativity going on, maybe they are not real, in the sense that they are not really real.

20 *The problem of performativity*

Both mundane and social-scientific accounts of derivative finance (and finance at large) tend to utilize the jargon of the virtual in order to deal with this (Carrier and Miller 1998; Knorr Cetina and Bruegger 2002). There is no doubt that financial derivatives partake of the virtual, but they do it in the Deleuzian, Bergsonian sense of the word (Deleuze 1966). This sense is complex; but, in short, it is explicit that 'virtual' is not synonymous with 'not real' – quite to the contrary. Alas, when the word is used to refer to finance, it often conveys a lack of reality, with financial objects, for instance, being less real than the objects of what has come to be referred to, strangely enough in my view, as the real economy. These widespread views clearly resonate with historical moments in which crises over the representation of the value of things in the economy have led to complex disquisitions on the links between markets and theatrical fiction (Shell 1982; Agnew 1986). I hope it is clear by now that the approach defended in these pages opposes this view. Descriptions are real. And financial objects, which are both descriptions and objects of description, are very, very real – which leads us to the problem of the simulacrum.

The problem of the simulacrum

Some very nasty philosophical pieces have been written about the simulacrum, especially in the face of contemporary media culture. Jean Baudrillard's opening remarks on the subject are rather devastating: 'Today, abstraction is no longer the abstraction of the map, of the double, of the mirror or of the concept. Simulation is no longer about a territory, about a referential being, about a substance. It is a model-generated real with no origin and no reality: hyperreal. The territory does not precede the map – *precession of simulacra* – it is the map that engenders the territory' (Baudrillard 1981: 10, my translation, his italics; see also Baudrillard 1994: 1).

Baudrillard added, 'In this shift to a space whose curvature is not that of reality, neither that of truth, the era of simulation opens with the liquidation of reference'; and 'It is about the substitution of reality with the signs of reality' (Baudrillard 1981: 11). This, of course, makes sense to a lot of readers. But it also resonates very much with the good old Platonic cavern, that is, with a standard philosophical take mostly characterized by annoyance at the distance that may exist between what one can access in terms or thought or perception and the real thing – more exactly, the idea. What one accesses is likely to be a copy instead of the original, or even a blatant, devilish falsification; hence, the discomfort.

But Baudrillard's is not the only possible perspective, and in the 1970s there was quite a lively entente on the non-Platonist view within French philosophical circles among people such as Pierre Klossowski, Michel Foucault and Gilles Deleuze on the problem of the simulacrum (e.g. Klossowski 1963; Foucault, 1964, 1970, 2011; Deleuze 1968a, 1969; Klossowski and Zucca 1970; for an overview see Smith 2005). For Deleuze, to put it bluntly, 'simulation refers to the power of producing an effect' (Deleuze 1969: 304, my translation). And effect – that is, effectuation – is the name of reality. Deleuze's investigation on the subject matter is in part an exploration of the alternatives that the stoics, for example, then Spinoza and then Nietzsche, would develop to counter the Platonic idea. A broad understanding of the psychoanalytic viewpoint did of course add consistency to this understanding of the reality of the simulacrum: the simulacrum is the vehicle for the realization of the act. In other words, the best way to love (or simply cope with) something is to do it; the simulacrum is about that precisely.

At this point, we are not too far removed from the discoveries of anthropology. We can easily remember the features of 'symbolic efficacy' (i.e. the pragmatic effectiveness of symbols) in shamanistic cure in the classic study by Claude Lévi-Strauss, where he developed an understanding of incantation (i.e. simulacrum) as a practical instrument for therapy (Lévi-Strauss 1949, for a pragmatist reading of Lévi-Strauss see Hennion 2010). Chants were first described as being used for 'psychological manipulation of the ill organ' (Lévi-Strauss 1949: 12, my translation), but then, as a way of 'introducing a series of events of which the body and the internal organs constitute the stage' (Lévi-Strauss 1949: 13). Very much like the psychoanalytical cure, Lévi-Strauss wrote, the shamanistic cure is about 'provoking an experience' (Lévi-Strauss 1949: 21) and therefore requires a broader, positive understanding of the notion of manipulation: 'It is sometimes about the manipulation of ideas, sometimes about the manipulation of organs, but in all cases through symbols, that is, through significant equivalents of what is signified, pertaining to a different order of reality' (Lévi-Strauss 1949: 22). Lévi-Strauss referred with admiration to Marguerite Sechehaye's psychoanalytic method of symbolic realization, which is a fundamental step in the psychotherapeutic understanding of the simulacrum (Sechehaye 1947). The name of the method says it all: the word 'realization' is certainly a more interesting translation of *Erfüllung* (Freud's *Wunscherfüllung*), than the usual 'fulfilment'.

Considering business organizations in the terms of the anthropology of remedial rituals is now perhaps a commonplace. The consultant as shaman or as witch doctor stands as a legitimate metaphor in the repertoire of business ethnography and also in the ordinary vocabulary of consultancy proper. Notions of incantation, storytelling and the manipulation of symbols populate both the critique of managerial culture and its ordinary practice (for a powerful landmark see Czarniawska 1997). The problem of the simulacrum can be dealt with, in these situations, through a rather discouraging angle inspired by Baudrillard (i.e. the lack of truthful reality within the manipulation of symbols in business remediation) or through a more Deleuzian movement, which I would like to call openly pragmatist (i.e. the realization of business through the business simulacrum). And the same can be said of many (if not all) other parts of economic life that require the intervention of simulacra.

Financial markets also provide a fertile test bed for the concept of the simulacrum. Schinckus (2008), for example, took Baudrillard's perspective, indicating that finance is hyperreal and leaving the reader with the impression that financial markets are not very real. However, Ellen Hertz (2000) had already delivered an extraordinarily accurate analysis of financial markets as simulacra which precisely aims at countering that bizarre impression. She observed how the notion of the simulacrum, which is implicitly at work in the critique of financial speculation (the compulsory reference to the proverbial beauty contest), is based on a Platonist, exacerbated focus on the problem of false representations as deceptive copies of the idea or, even worse, as copies of nothing. But an alternative exists. Following Latour (1991, 1993a), Hertz went on to establish a general philosophy of translation for the understanding of financial objects. From this perspective, what indeed exists and is real is the network of translations that develops at the surface of representations, in a world that is only constituted by what happens at its surface (which is a Deleuzian formulation). Hence, the positive reality of the simulacrum is considered to be the very stuff (both social and material) that constitutes finance. Indeed, Hertz called the stock market a 'community of effects' (Hertz 1998: 28, 2000: 49).

The problem of provocation

I have just emphasized the importance of effect and effectuation in understanding a performative take on reality. To have an effect is to provoke, to be an effect is a provocation of reality. Needless to say, the vocabulary of provocation resonates in philosophy with Martin Heidegger's *Herausfordern* (Heidegger 1958). Broadly speaking, technology, Heideggerian readers would gather, is not only constituted by instrumental devices. It is also a particular way of considering (or 'unveiling') what is. My apologies for the metaphysical jargon, but we are confronted here with the problem of being, more exactly of its predication. Technology considers what is, but does so in a particular manner – specifically, through provocation. Technology provokes what is. Of course, in Heideggerian terms this is said with some discouragement, since what is should be contemplated, rather than provoked. The comparison would be with some more noble ways of considering what is: that of the poet, for example. A far less reactionary, more realistic and perhaps even more poetic way of tackling technology can be found in Bruno Latour's pragmatist take on technology. There is disagreement on this claim (Harman 2009; Kochan 2010), but after having read Heidegger's piece on the question of technique, I agree with Latour's perspective.

Latour's notion of the experimental event is essential here (Latour 1999: 113–44, see also Latour 1990, 1993b). An experiment is an event in the sense that it provokes a new articulation. It cannot be accounted for through a list of its intervening actors (its ingredients), because the competence of intervening actors (i.e. their acting capacity) is '*acquired in the event*' (Latour 1999: 126, his emphasis). Actors, which are basically no more and no less than lists of effects (i.e. 'performances', in Latour's words), emerge as such within and throughout an event, which is a trial on agency (Latour 1999: 308). The philosophical problem is, again, that of reality as performed reality. The Latourian answer to the question 'Are provoked things real?' would be a resounding 'Well, look around you!' and here, perhaps, the bridge with the Heideggerian standpoint becomes more tenable. To this add the problem of the provoker, and here we can again rely on the down-to-earth empirical description that Latour provided of Louis Pasteur and his lactic acid ferment: 'We need to understand that whatever we want to think or argue about the artificial character of the laboratory, or the literary aspects of this particular type of exegesis, the lactic acid ferment is *not* invented by Pasteur but *by the ferment*' (Latour 1999: 124, his emphasis). Provocation is immanent to the event; the demiurge is inside the thing, not outside. We should note in this regard Latour's sympathy to hylozoism and to ecological theology (Latour 2009, 2010a; Latour *et al.* 2011).

Provocation also means challenge, and, as Javier Izquierdo would have had it, the notion calls for some sympathy for the metaphysical value of the prank (Izquierdo 2004; Muniesa 2011b). It is common sense – well, it should be – to claim that experimental sciences account for what they provoke, and that the form of knowledge they constitute is absolutely performative in that sense (Lezaun *et al.* 2013). It is also common sense to argue that since they provoke things, precautions in terms of ethics apply. The history of clinical trials and biomedical investigation provides a long record of evidence in this respect, and so does the history of experimental methods in the social sciences (see Korn 1997; Keating and Cambrosio 2003; Brannigan 2004; Will and Moreira 2010). What is perhaps less expected is to talk here about pranks. But if one looks for example at the scientific ethos of Stanley Milgram, known for reporting on the most shocking social-scientific revelations and also for being an admirer of Allen Funt's *Candid Camera* (the popular reality television show), one can see the interest in the parallel (Blass 2004; McCarthy 2004). The hidden camera prank is a perfect model of the fundamental problem of provocation. It intensifies both the revelatory power of experimental orchestration and its generative thrill. It problematizes reality.

The problem of explicitness

Provoking, effecting, performing something is a way of exposing it to consideration. It is a way, in other words, of making something explicit. Here again we hit upon a well-known philosophical problem, because saying that something is being made explicit can very well mean that the thing was there already, implicit, existing in a latent, veiled, secret or potential form, for instance, in the form of an idea. On the other hand, one can claim that explicitness is a quite demanding state to be in, which affects what is at stake in a truly inventive fashion, with no particularly transcendental antecedent. I think that the very mundane idea of being explicit about something – being called to make a clearer and more detailed statement about something that was initially formulated in rather loose terms or only in terms of general principles – rather supports the latter claim. (Writing these pages is a good example.) A call for explicitness rarely translates into the unproblematic unfolding of one single programme that may have already been settled in an implicit or latent form. On the contrary, a call for explicitness often translates into the emergence of grey areas, the discovery of new problems and, sometimes, the development of controversies about what exactly is to be made explicit and how. In a sense, many of the types of practices pertaining to the world of postmodern knowledge in the sense of Lyotard (1984) are characterized by a recurrent exposure to what I call trials of explicitness (e.g. in operations research, accounting, finance, audit or management).

But the philosophical debate is not settled, and the concept of explication (*explicatio* in Latin, perhaps best translated as *Explikation* in German, or *explicitation* in French) is a tricky one that is also linked in a rather complex way to the concept of expression. The notion conveys, of course, something of an idea of unfolding, of deploying, of opening up (opening the fold, the *pli*), as opposed, for instance, to an idea of folding, or of complicating. But it is not very clear what this may mean, and the philosophical problem of explication is an open one. Of particular interest, for instance, is the question of how prefigured (i.e. how ideated) the thing is that undergoes explication. Is explication about the laborious unveiling (or the working out) of something that is already there, implicit? Or is it a creative, performative, generative, provocative process that adds more reality to reality? And is it about the breath of intelligence tackling an initially chaotic matter and making it meaningful (*pneuma* over *plasma*)? Or is it rather about a seamless play of folding and unfolding in a world which is constituted only by what happens at its surface?

A possible inclination for the second view in these two sets of questions is visible in a number of philosophical traditions which have been emphasized, for example (but not only), by Gilles Deleuze (1966, 1968a, 1968b, 1969, 1988a; translated respectively as 1988b, 1994, 1990b, 1990a, 1993). My rough summary of Deleuze's perspective on this follows. To make something explicit (or, for that matter, to explicate it or express it, although there are conceptual subtleties in vocabulary that I am just ignoring here) is not about clarifying what remains obscure or about realizing what is prefigured. There is some realization going on throughout explicitness, of course, in both the sense of making something real and in understanding it. It may seem as though a two-layer situation exists, with things that are ready to be realized on top (e.g. in the form of ideas), and things that are ready for actual implementation below, which themselves are more or less felicitous. But that is just an impression. Explicitness is the state in which things are tested within their own type of reality. And there is only one layer, one surface, in which things proliferate, some of which lack some

26 *The problem of performativity*

bits of reality (i.e. are virtual) and are less constrained. Some virtual objects, like the phallus to name one at random, exist as witnesses of their own absence (Deleuze 1968a: 136, 1994: 103). The economy, the economic object, would be another virtual object in the sense that it becomes explicit throughout the test of actual implementation (Deleuze 1968a: 241, 1994: 186).

This goes hand in hand with the sort of industrial ontology that Bruno Latour has developed for the social sciences. It is interesting to note that Latour himself has been seduced by the notion of explicitness, although the notion of articulation is more appropriately developed in his writings. He has often signalled, for instance, Peter Sloterdijk's use of the notion of *Explikation* to refer to the anthropological revolution introduced by gas warfare, air conditioning and comparable technologies in the early twentieth century. These technologies engage in a process of explicating the atmospheric conditions of breathability and subsistence, and in so doing, contribute to the constitution of a world characterized by the continuous extension, provocation and exacerbation of these conditions (Latour 2006, 2010b; Sloterdijk 2009a, 2009b). But the notion of explicitness, as developed here, could perhaps be used more effectively to highlight one of Latour's more crucial contributions to the discussion of constructivism: namely, his commentary on Ramses II (Latour 2000). The death of the pharaoh can be explicated today in the terms of Koch's bacillus, and the statement 'Ramses II died of tuberculosis' can be true, but at a cost. This ontological work of explication goes unnoticed epistemologically when one forgets to look into the networks of the production of reality, which is typical when these networks have been collapsed into what Latour calls 'black boxes'. Should we remind ourselves here that the pharaoh's own religion was a craft of the performative (Assmann 1992)?

Description, simulacrum, provocation and explicitness: we end up here with four challenges, four lineaments to which I say we should commit if we want to face the performative turn with more than a good intention and a vague impression. We are quite far away from any idea of thoughts having effects on things, of theories having an impact on practices, of principles informing particulars, of representations influencing whatever it is that it is represented. We depart from the two-layer setting in which that would make sense. There is only one layer – a cracked, filamentous and turbulent layer, bumpy and shaggy, but quite horizontal. This setting might not be very comfortable, but taking the performative turn from here is the starting point of a serious, yet surprising, enquiry. Where shall we go from here? The economy is not just one possible destination among others. It is perhaps the site in which the two-layered view is more vividly articulated, and more resilient; the medium in which modernity is ultimately plunged. It quite deserves to be approached through a performative angle, but it also promises a difficult journey.

2 The consideration of economic reality

Let us now approach the subject of the economy proper. The problem of performativity in economic reality has been addressed in a variety of styles and ways. A list-like review of the literature broadly reveals narratives of economic rationalization and capitalistic development, philosophical interpretations of economic institutions, studies on the use and effects of economic sciences, critical accounts of the history and operation of the notion of the economy, sociological analyses of the practices of marketing, and investigations on management and accounting at work. Once acknowledged, we can allow ourselves to enter into a more analytic, deeper discussion on two topics that I think still require some work: the naturalness of economic things in the tradition of modern economic reason and the pragmatic meaning of the action of economization – two crucial problems confronted when considering economic reality in performative terms.

Studies in the constitution of economic things

Perhaps it should be made clear from the outset that discussing performativity in the economy is more than discussing the performativity of economics and that numerous perspectives have been taken on the problem, which is not new. In what follows, I briefly mention a number of viewpoints, traditions and specialities that have contributed, with their own vocabularies and concerns, crucial elements to the broad topic of how economic things are provoked. Please note that they all connect to each other, and that this is not an exhaustive review. Rather, these perspectives offer points of reference that are instrumental for the type of reflection that is being done here in this book.

Critique of economic rationalization

The fact that the configuration of an economic world results, at least in part, from the implementation of a number of economic techniques has been well established in the classics of political economy and social theory alike. Take, for example, how Karl Marx considered capital not as a thing in itself but as a form, as a way to configure a social relation of production, or more exactly as a way, first, to formally describe that relation in capitalistic terms, and second, to enter into the process of so-called real subsumption, a process in which labour is indeed effectively organized in order to conform to those terms (Godelier 1990). To subsume is, in a sense, to perform. Consider also the topic of economic rationalization as put forward, for example, in the sociology of Max Weber or, more narrowly, the debates on the (let us say performative) role of accounting techniques such as double-entry bookkeeping in the development of the capitalist, the capitalist's conduct, and capitalism, as both a reality and a concept (see Chiapello 2007). Think also, for example, about Karl Polanyi and his more recent critique of the self-regulating market, its academic incantations, and the devices of its implementation, properly performative devices in an open sense of the word (for an update, see Hahn and Hart 2009). The classical critique (be it socialist or otherwise) of economic rationality has been historically attentive to the intellectual flaws of the unabashed sciences of the economy, but also (perhaps more interestingly) to the practical vehicles through which a certain kind of economic rationality was becoming instituted. Contemporary accounts of financialization, liberalization, globalization and domination in economic life are generally attentive to this (see for example Fligstein 1990; Roy 1997; Froud *et al.* 2006; Nitzan and Bichler 2009; Krippner 2011). In many (most) accounts, there is indeed the idea that formulating reality in capitalistic terms might, in some circumstances, transform the formulated reality.

The interpretation of economic institutions

The task of interrogating the categories of knowledge with attention to the institutions they require in terms of veridiction (i.e. how truth is told) is often linked to Michel Foucault. His own engagement with the topic of the economy, most notably in his 1977–8 and 1978–9 lectures at the Collège de France, is explicitly an enquiry into the morphology of liberalism: its intellectual morphology and the morphology of its translation into apparatuses of government (Foucault 2004a, 2004b, translated into English in 2007, 2008). Governing, conducting and controlling are all things that, within the scope of liberalism, are accomplished through the elaboration of economic categories: the apparition of the economic as a distinct order of measure, the construction of the economy as the proper object of political government, the instillation of entrepreneurship as the model of the subject. His detailed analysis of, for example, the meandering development of neoliberal economic doctrines in the construction of the post-World War II German social market economy put Foucault at the forefront of historical examinations of the influence of neoliberal thought (see also Davies 2009; Mirowski and Plehwe 2009). But his philosophical depth and his commitment to the interpretation of veridiction as a contingent process put him also at the forefront of the philosophical anthropology that has been struggling to elucidate the production of modern ideology, alongside, for example, Louis Dumont and his study of individualism (Dumont 1983, translated as 1986). Foucauldian or near-Foucauldian analyses do hence contribute insistently, through a variety of angles, to an understanding of the constitution of economic things (Burchell *et al.*1991; Barry *et al.*1996; Miller and Rose 2008).

The efficacy of economics

Historians, sociologists and anthropologists of science and technology (or at least those acquainted with these subjects) have contributed consistently to our understanding of the role of economics in the constitution and transformation of economic things. The empirical investigations of Donald MacKenzie and Yuval Millo on the history of pricing models and the construction of North American markets for financial derivative contracts constitute a remarkable contribution in this line of enquiry (MacKenzie 2003, 2004, 2006; MacKenzie and Millo 2003; Millo 2007; Millo and MacKenzie 2009). Javier Izquierdo's earlier contribution was also pivotal in the establishment of this speciality in the social studies of finance (Izquierdo 2001; see also Izquierdo Martín 1996). Here, the constitution of economic things (tradable financial derivatives) is tackled from the angle of the specialized forms of science that they mobilize, and also of the foreseen and unforeseen characteristics of their behaviour. As these studies have become crucial in our understanding of the sociology of derivatives trading, the topic of the performativity of economics has become indeed one persistent ingredient of the social studies of finance (De Goede 2005; Langley 2008; Preda 2009).

But these and comparable perspectives have been used to confront other subjects. The power of resource economics in the framing of environmental policy has been scrutinized, for instance, in the case of markets for transferable quotas in fisheries (Holm and Nolde Nielsen 2007) or in the case of emissions trading and carbon offsetting (Callon 2009; Lohmann 2009; MacKenzie 2009), and the list does not stop there. A variety of industrial sectors have been studied from a similar point of view (e.g. Dumez and Jeunemaître 1998). Work from notable contributors to the history or sociology of science have illuminated topics such as the constitution of macroeconomic science and macroeconomic policy (e.g. Evans 1997, 1999a, 1999b; Hecht 1998; Breslau and Yonay 1999; Morgan and Den Butter 2000; Breslau 2005; Armatte 2010). Overall, studies on the performativity of economics have almost found their way into the social-scientific mainstream (for an assessment see MacKenzie *et al.* 2007; Muniesa and Callon 2009).

Empires, nations, colonies, economies

Timothy Mitchell is perhaps among the most visible advocates of the study of the economy as both an artefact of and vehicle for colonial and neocolonial ventures. In his work on Egypt (Mitchell 1991, 1998, 2002), he examined the invention of the Egyptian national economy, that is, the technical work that enabled this entity to be brought into existence and acted upon from a distance. This was entirely about making the Egyptian national economy explicit, visible and actionable, for instance, through a statistical treatment of a very particular form: that of an economic space characterized by a problem of economic resources in need of international economic expertise from the International Monetary Fund, the World Bank and the US Agency for International Development, in particular. Mitchell added to a growing set of analyses that have examined the role of economic expertise in the construction of national economic spaces in South America, Africa, Asia and Eastern Europe (Valdés 1995; Bockman and Eyal 2002; Dezalay and Garth 2002; Babb 2004; Goswami 2004; Elyachar 2005). Mitchell's more recent analyses of neoliberal recipes against poverty in developing countries (Mitchell 2005, 2007, 2008) and the strategies of oil economics (2009, 2010) also provide remarkable illustrations of the role played by the performance of economic things in the construction of political empires. As a general rule, when the behaviour of a human collective is referred to as the behaviour of its economy, and when its identity is assimilated to the perimeter of its economic space, we are witnessing an outstanding achievement in the constitution of a collective as an economic (or economized) resource.

The arts of marketing and the crafts of elicitation

The emerging field of the social studies of marketing (see in particular Callon *et al.* 2007; Araujo *et al.* 2010; Zwick and Cayla 2011) can be defined as having a shared interest in how specialities such as marketing, market research, branding and advertising shape (purposefully, most of the time) the things they target – specifically, consumers. In this type of literature, it is widely acknowledged that the consumer is a persona essentially pertaining to the marketing text; features such as consumer preferences are mostly enacted within the market research setting; and consumer behaviour is an artefact of the corresponding market device (see the pioneering work of Cochoy 1999, 2002). Of course, this does not mean that consumers do not exist and that marketing is a fiction. The proper word here is, again, effectuation.

Take, for instance, the case of the focus group, the proverbial market research setting that originated in the laboratory of experimental social research (Merton and Kendall 1946; Merton 1987). As Lezaun (2007a) and Grandclément and Gaglio (2011) have established, the type of reality signified within a focus group is very artificial, the elicitation of opinions is constructed and, still, the 'focus group effect' (as Catherine Grandclément and Gérald Gaglio call it) is precisely that of producing the persona of the consumer in front of the marketing clients, that is, a performance of the elicitation of consumer talk. We are most certainly tackling here one of the most intriguing instances of the simulacrum in the construction of markets and in the fabrication of consumer culture. Research on these types of topics has been populating in a quite creative way in literature in the so-called area of cultural economy (Du Gay and Pryke 2002; Amin and Thrift 2004; McFall 2004; Hetherington 2007; Lash and Lury 2007). And this whole area of study is indeed prime ground for examination of the provoked economy.

Managerial and accountancy settings

Sites of organized economic labour constitute the theatre of a number of events and situations that are likely to be analysed in terms of performativity: slideshow presentations in strategic management, the publication of accounting spreadsheets, acts of audit and verification, the introduction of performance indicators, demonstrations of new information systems, and presentations of business models and business plans. An immense literature in accounting and management studies explicitly tackles these with attention to the apparatuses that are mobilized, the rituals that are developed and the effects that are produced. The performance of slideshow presentations, for example, has been examined by Sarah Kaplan (2011) in quite a remarkable manner (see also Yates and Orlikowski 2007; Beaudoin 2008; Knoblauch 2008; Stark and Paravel 2008; Gaglio 2009), and Liliana Doganova and Marie Eyquem-Renault (2009) have discussed business models with explicit reference to performativity (see also Giraudeau 2008; Baden-Fuller and Morgan 2010; Perkmann and Spicer 2010).

Likewise, the constructive, performative features of representational practices constitute a topic of acknowledged relevance in accounting studies (Hopwood and Miller 1994; Power 1996). It is unsurprising that one can observe the extent to which the distinctive vocabulary of actor–network theory has penetrated the accounting literature (e.g. Robson 1991, 1992). Paolo Quattrone's investigation on the bodily and mental practice of bookkeeping provides quite a neat understanding of what performativity can mean in such contexts: the production of facts and, at the same time, lasting realization of such facts (Quattrone 2009). Researchers concerned by these types of objects and assembled in areas commonly known as accounting studies, management studies or organization studies are what Bruno Latour called – probably without their consent but in a positive way, and with very explicit indications for their taste for the performative – the 'flat-earthers' of social sciences (Latour 1996). Flat indeed is the world they study, great social wholes being considered as performative achievements rather than as ultimate explanatory forces.

The anthropology of the economic

Another large portion of the social sciences that is instrumental in understanding the constitution of economic things is economic anthropology (and economic sociology of the qualitative, interpretive kind). Maurice Godelier (1965) considered, quite appropriately, the subject of economic anthropology not as an economic subject per se, but as a particular aspect (an economic one, related to the production, allocation and consumption of goods) that any situation may have. For example, such aspects of a Mozart recital would be the price of the ticket and the payment to the artist, but not the beauty of the music (Godelier 1965: 38). But, as Godelier himself observed, this economic

34 The problem of performativity

aspect is related to other aspects and is also quite difficult to delineate in a systematic manner. In fact, one could say that this is precisely the anthropological point: to study how this delineation is done in practice.

Studies of how economic aspects of social life express themselves combine in economic anthropology with studies of how other aspects of social life are made economic. Particularly illuminating examinations of the constitution of economic things can, for instance, be found in the work of Viviana Zelizer on economic transactions related to children or sex (Zelizer 1985, 2005; see also Zelizer 1997, 2010). A sexual encounter, for instance, can be considered in certain circumstances as a biological event (an encounter between cells) or as an affective event (an encounter between affectively connected persons), but the economic anthropologist would examine it as an economic event (an exchange between parties). Studies of popular economic practices in Africa have been particularly attentive to the performative aspects of economic calculation, as put forward, for example, in the work of Jane Guyer (Guyer 2004; see also Maurer 2007; Roitman 2007; Verran 2007; Guyer 2009, 2010; Lépinay and Callon 2009). Observations of how financial objects are described and constituted as financial have benefited from lessons on the anthropology of Islamic banking provided, for example, by Bill Maurer (2002a, 2002b, 2005) – and these are just a few examples. From the anthropological understanding of an economic transaction as a performance, very much in the theatrical sense of the word, to anthropological observations of how economic sciences and techniques frame economic reality, the performativity of economic acts appears as an explicit concern in the anthropological literature.

And more

As the reader can see from this brief summary, the topic of the constitution of economic things (the topic of the provoked economy) is served by a vast landscape of efforts. A rigorous review requires acknowledging contributions from theories of reflexive modernity (e.g. Lamo de Espinosa 1990; Beck *et al.*1994), the history of calculation (e.g. Desrosières 1993, 1998; Crosby 1997), geography (e.g. Leyshon and Thrift 1997; Barry 2001; Thrift 2005), critical legal studies (e.g. Nader 2002; Mattei and Nader 2008; Gerber 2010), feminist economics (e.g. Ferber and Nelson 1993; Gibson-Graham 1996), environmentalist critique (e.g. Gould *et al.* 2008), the sociology of the economic field (e.g. Bourdieu 2000, 2005; Fourcade 2009), new institutionalism in sociology (e.g. Powell and DiMaggio 1991), critical institutionalism in economics (e.g. Aglietta 1976; Boyer 1990; Lordon 1997, 2002), and more. My purpose here is not to present a stable field, but simply to show that we are not alone. Of course, the intuition of performativity may not be spelled out at all in these lines of enquiry, with authors favouring theoretical vocabularies more adapted to their particular endeavours and preferences. My point is not that they share or should share an underlying understanding. I only indicate that any clear attempt at considering economic reality as a provoked reality requires close examination of all of them. But this is only part of the job. There are a few problems that still require fresh attention.

Economic naturalism against the practice of economizing

As the second part of the previous chapter dealt with some problems of performativity in general, so does this one. Here, I narrow the discussion to performativity in economic matters and focus on two specific problems, which are highly problematic. The first is related to the modern science of the economy and its particular blend of naturalism. The second is related to the possibility of establishing a useful, pragmatist definition of what it is to make something economic or to economize something.

The problem with modern economic reason

In his lectures at the Collège de France (the inaugural lecture was given on 16 January 2001), Ian Hacking developed the idea of styles of reasoning in order to scrutinize the different ways in which sense is made and truth is considered in the sciences (Hacking 2002a, 2002b; Kusch 2010). In the summer of 2006, at the Colloque de Cerisy organized by Bruno Latour and Philippe Descola on the topic of the historical anthropology of scientific reason (12–19 July 2006), Hacking's ideas, together with those of other notable contributors to the history of science such as Lorraine Daston, Peter Galison, Hans-Jörg Rheinberger and Isabelle Stengers, were exposed to Philippe Descola's newly formalized structural anthropology of the different modes of identification of beings, or, in other words, of the varieties of cosmology or methods of intellection in humankind (Descola 2005, 2013), also developed in the same period in the form of lectures at the Collège de France. Almost all historians of science and anthropologists gathered at the Château de Cerisy-La-Salle (the exalted venue of the Colloque de Cerisy) were of course familiar with naturalism as one defining anthropological feature of the style of reasoning, or the mode of identification of beings, in modern science.

In Descola's terms, naturalism is a structure of intellection characterized by a univocal and external nature: there might be several interiorities, preferably human (i.e. human subjects), but all beings (including, but not only, human beings) share a similar physicality. However, this is absolutely not the case for other perspectives, structurally defined as totemist, animist or analogist in Descola's typology (see also Descola 1996; Viveiros de Castro 1998, 2004). The crucial hypothesis shared at the Colloque de Cerisy was of course that the particular style of Western modern reason is plainly naturalistic. The modern scientist can talk about multiculturalism (several cultures, several ways of thinking and of seeing things, several ways of experiencing human interiority), but never about multinaturalism (since there is only one nature). Human beings are strictly distinguished from other beings. They distinguish themselves because they have one kind of interiority that we call subjectivity and which might be idiosyncratic. But they all share among them and with other beings a similar physicality, in the sense that they share the same laws of nature. Bodies are bodies here and elsewhere. Molecules are molecules here and elsewhere. Radiation is radiation here and elsewhere. The self-evident outcome of that state of mind is modern scientific enquiry. Galileo's motto is crucial in this characterization of naturalism: the book of nature might not be easy to read, but there is surely only one and it is written in mathematical language, i.e. a language prone to scientific reading.

Authors such as Bruno Latour, however, have meticulously opposed this version of what modern thought is and how it operates (Latour 1993a). For Latour, naturalism corresponds to the picture modern science keenly provides of itself, but is at odds with what modern science really does. According to Latour, the archetypical modern thinker speaks with a forked tongue, praising naturalism, pretending to be a naturalistic-minded enquirer, but in practice failing to refrain from producing hybrids between nature and culture, and continuing to be entirely performative. Such duplicitous behaviours constitute probably the main outcome of the symmetric anthropology of modern reason undertaken by Bruno Latour. Economic reason is perhaps the toughest and gravest chapter in Latour's philosophical anthropology (Latour 2012: 381–471).

How does modern economic reason, or the modern science of the economy, fit into this? Is naturalism a fundamental characteristic of economic thought? Or is it an instance, perhaps the grossest one, of the modern forked tongue? It is easy to recognize in economics a sort of naturalistic style: we may all have different cultures, opinions and beliefs, but we all share the same economic laws. Money is money here and elsewhere. Budgetary constraints are budgetary constraints here and elsewhere. Marginal utility is marginal utility here and elsewhere. We may all have different preferences, but we all certainly have such a thing as 'economic preferences' that can be taken into account economically and aggregated together into some sort of an economic calculation. Any sort of process, regardless of its particular point and scope, as soon as it is costly (and any process may be costly) is economic in nature and thus prone to economic analysis (see Godelier 1965: 35–6). Economic characteristics characterize not only individuals, but also groups, families, countries and firms, as well as natural resources, ecosystems, animals or, by extension, cells, neurons, machines and computer programs. This seems naturalistic indeed: a reason that goes through all and unifies all, an economic nature that is transversal to all bodies and to all souls. Is economic reason the paramount naturalistic reason?

The history of ideas has explored at length naturalistic style in economic reason, with special attention to the construction of the categories of modern economics, starting with the notion of the economic individual, the notion of self-interest, the notion of utility and so forth, including also the study of how mathematics and formalistic languages in general have allowed economics to be emancipated, as a science, from moral philosophy and to proceed to study economic laws as natural laws (see, for instance, Mirowski 1989; Ingrao and Israel 1990; Dumont 1983; Dupuy 1992a; Demeulenaere 1996; Laval 2007; Sahlins 2008). Do note also that the object of enquiry in this particular science, especially in its contemporary form, is a transversal object, an object often placed beyond the boundary between the social sciences and the natural sciences. Note how difficult it is for economists to consider their science as a 'social' science. This 'general' object – economic processes – is quite comparable to the equally general and transversal object – information – that pioneering cybernetics focused on (Mirowski 2002). Note also how the sometimes openly abstract and minimalist character of economic models can be criticized on the grounds of their scholastic illusions (Bourdieu 1997, 2000, 2005), but also openly justified on the grounds that the ambition of economic theory would not be to exactly describe what happens in the real world, but to isolate and comprehend a mechanism that is almost impossible to isolate in the wild, to abstract it, to simulate it, to create what Nancy Cartwright has called a 'nomological machine' (Cartwright 1999). Note finally how having practical effects, fostering policy implications and achieving economic realizations is frequently put forward in economics as a correlate of being right – definitely not as some sort of contradiction.

Michel Callon's position on the performativity of economics (Callon 1998, 2007) has generated epistemic discomfort among some critics of economics precisely because the ultimate, quite naturalistic, epistemic critique – that of accusing a body of science of being wrong – is jeopardized within the performative idiom (e.g. Mirowski and Nik-Khah 2007). The paradox (not to say the pity) is that a critique of economics that is uncomfortable with performativity has to claim, first, that economics does not matter (literally, since as such it does not provoke anything) and, second, that it needs to be criticized anyway. But why should we waste time criticizing something that does not matter? Economists themselves tend rather not to care about the discussion, finding it perhaps abstruse and irrelevant, or just candidly conceding that there is nothing wrong with being performative when it is done well (e.g. Colander 2008). Some naturalistic style intervenes at the surface of economics, but the hypothesis of the modern forked tongue (claiming naturalism while blatantly performing) applies also quite well to the case of economic reason: performative pride, wrapped up into a naturalistic epistemological layer. When you say that the book of nature is written in economic language but then you get caught in the act with that book in one hand and a pen in the other, the wisest thing to do is probably to smile at the camera and say that, yes, you were writing it but you were writing it well.

To economize, to abstract, to value, to capitalize

There is a problem, then, with modern economic reason and one prominent aspect of the problem is the difficulty of coping with performativity from a naturalist, modernistic perspective. The option, I think, is to abandon that perspective. But let us now leave the cloudy realm of the anthropology of modern thought to tackle again the study of economic, organized reality. The pragmatist question could be formulated as follows: is economic reality a type of reality, or is it an economic type of effect? In clear resonance with what has been said previously, both here and elsewhere (see also Barry 2002; Law 2002; Muniesa *et al.* 2007; Çalışkan and Callon 2009, 2010; Muniesa 2010, 2012, 2013), 'the economic' is indeed perhaps best considered as an action, an action of economizing, which is, pragmatically speaking, an action of signifying economically – definitely not a realm, a domain or a principle. Things can be economized.

But what does this signify? Of course, the idea of what 'economic' means here is prone to multiple interpretations. To make something economic can be one or several of the following things (among others): to put a price on it, to sell or buy it, to produce it for exchange, to hoard or to ration it, to make it commensurable, to consider it as an asset, to regard it as scarce or costly, to spend or consume it, to treat is as part of a system or circuit, to allocate or administer it, to speculate on it, to use it as a lever, to assess its efficiency, to finance it. The particulars should be left to the empirics of actual, situated configurations. It is indeed quite clear that very different penchants for economizing will be displayed in domestic housekeeping, Soviet planning, investment banking, management accounting or ceremonial gift-giving. Economization does not have only one colour. But it is, however, a kind of movement that is identifiable as such. How?

The common feature would be perhaps an inherent exacerbation of the calculative articulation of things, in one way or another: division and subtraction (i.e. rationing), and multiplication and addition (i.e. leveraging). Studies on the visual, diagrammatic features of economic computation such as, for example, the work of Paolo Quattrone on the visual craft of early accounting (Quattrone 2009; see also Crosby 1997), remind us that *ratio* (Latin for reason, but more exactly for calculation and computation) is about drawing a material line, about performing a displacement, about cutting things, about paying, as does a non-metaphorical understanding of the vocabulary of *rationem putare* and *summa* (Benveniste 1969: vol. I, 151–4, 1973; see also Callon and Muniesa 2005: 1231).

As a material movement (a performance), the act of economizing resembles another: that of abstracting. Abstraction has been at the centre of many analyses of monetary mediations, mercantile enterprises and capitalistic forms (Maurer 2006). One usual way of phrasing what economizing is about is indeed to say that it is about abstracting, although this act of abstracting is of course not exclusive to economic undertakings. Abstraction here needs to be considered as a verb (a performance) rather than as a noun. Abstraction, or rather to abstract, is an action, an action of transformation and displacement, as in 'to extract' or 'to draw away' suggested by its etymology: *abs* (away), *trahere* (tract). To a large extent, to abstract something is to transport it into a formal, calculative space (Callon and Muniesa 2005). Economic arrangements are cluttered with a variety of abstractive calculative devices: pricing techniques, accounting methods, monitoring instruments, trading protocols and benchmarking procedures are abstractors that enter into the construction of the economic. Economists too are abstractive agencies: they calculate aggregates, they produce formal models or metric configurations that can be, almost by definition, parts of economic arrangements. To abstract is to make the economic portable.

Valuing is a third kind of movement that is worthwhile to consider here, along with economizing and abstracting. From the pragmatist perspective put forward by authors such as John Dewey, the intellectual problem of value (whether it is objective or subjective, and so forth) could be better approached through a 'flank movement' which basically consists in abandoning value as a substantive feature and considering valuation as an empirical act (Dewey 1939; see also Muniesa 2012). The establishment of networks of valuation (in the material semiotic sense of 'network' developed in actor–network theory) is what, for example, markets are about (Muniesa 2007, 2012). But immersing things in networks of valuation is not only about considering these things from an economic viewpoint. It is first and foremost about getting these things actively prepared for an economic act (e.g. the act of selling or purchasing, the act of investing).

Capitalizing, a fourth movement worth considering as part of a convenient vocabulary for the social studies of economic organizing, is an intensified, deeply oriented, and highly generative form of valuation. In a sense, the semiotic interpretation of capital that Félix Guattari and Gilles Deleuze tried to develop in their joint venture (Deleuze and Guattari 1972, 1980, translated in 1983, 1987; see also Guattari 2011) pointed towards the possibility of considering capitalization as a material, performative act of interpreting economic things. Capitalization is the reduction of a stream of future earnings to their present value through the use of a calculative device (a discount rate) which signals how much a capitalist would be prepared to pay to receive a future flow of money. But capitalization is capitalization of something, which translates into power for the capitalist over the thing undergoing capitalization (Nitzan and Bichler 2009). As a particular form of writing, of encoding (Guattari and Alliez 1983, 1984), capitalization is a type of valuation that organizes things as vehicles for investment – vehicles for the production of money with money.

What I hope now is that further elaborations of the performative perspective on the 'provoked economy' will allow me, as well as others, to venture further in the immediate future into a pragmatic enquiry into what it takes to economize, abstract, value and capitalize on things. The following snapshots are suggestions about what can be done with the intuitions briefly sketched out in the preceding pages. Understanding operations of economization, abstraction, valuation and capitalization – and many other types of operations that enter into the constitution of economic realities – as performative operations is not easy and will require, as we shall see, empirical attention to the intricacies of description, the procedures of simulacrum, the crafts of provocation and the manoeuvres of explicitness.

Part II
Elementary case studies

3 Recounting financial objects

What is investment banking about, apart from about making money with money, which it is, of course? If one looks at the activities carried out in the trading rooms of large international investment banks, one notices how prevalent the problem of description is. Investment banking is about describing financial products, writing them, checking their terms, re-describing them in different terms, forwarding and verifying these descriptions, making sense (especially financial sense) of them. This is even more visible when one examines the locus of the paperwork: that is, the back office. In this chapter I briefly take the reader through the intricacies of description in the back office division of an international investment bank. I draw mainly from fieldwork interviews with staff conducted in 2003; aspects of this research have already been published elsewhere (Muniesa *et al.* 2011). The fieldwork materials are quite old, but the problems are not. If you were to step into that bank today you would encounter pretty much the same puzzles that were visible there 10 years ago. The point here, however, is not to provide an informed clarification of what is going on in the back office department of a large, international investment bank. It is rather to flesh out, empirically, the problem of the description of financial objects: what it means and how it can be understood.

The investment bank as a puzzle

In his ethnography of financial engineering in an international investment bank, Vincent-Antonin Lépinay (2007a, 2007b, 2011) observed two important things. First, he remarked that complex financial products call for a fine-grained articulation of several languages: mathematical, commercial, legal, computational, and so forth. Lépinay focused on particularly complicated financial objects: 'formula' products, that is, derivative contracts with complex clauses and multiple pricing parameters. This work of articulation consists in 'the adjustment of all sorts of linguistic codes to express a novel, not-yet-described product' (Lépinay 2007a: 88). Here, at least in my understanding, 'express' and 'not-yet-described' do not mean that the product is already there, fully formed – potentially at least – waiting to be used, explained, forwarded, traded, hedged, implemented and described. Expression and description (to that end, two different names for the same process), or articulation, as Lépinay preferred following Latour (1999), is the ontological work that ends up forming these products or, as Lépinay himself wrote, granting them with liquidity. The second important thing that Lépinay observed is that problems of articulation often crystallize in back office organizational apparatuses, which are there in part to resolve ambiguities and discrepancies in the description of financial objects, that is, in 'keeping track' of them (Lépinay 2007b: 266–8, 271–5). This is indeed comparable to what happens at Thoth Bank.

Thoth Bank is the fictional name of a non-fictional investment bank, a quite large one. As many investment banks, it has a type of national allegiance, but is also recognized as a reputable player in all corners of the financial globe. Like the one investigated by Lépinay, it is marked by a heavy culture of financial innovation and is well known in the international milieus of risk sophistication. At Thoth Bank, the whole business of finance seems to be haunted by problems related to the description of financial objects: descriptions of products and their constitutive parts, their behaviour, the trades in which they are involved and the counterparties participating in them; descriptions of the settlement circuits and marketplace environments through which they move; descriptions of the profits and losses they generate. This is a story of sense-making. Thoth Bank asks – must ask – what is going on, what is it doing and where, perhaps also what for, but surely and definitely what and for how much. Of course, this is in part a story of employees trying to make sense of their activities inside the organization, a story of people narrating their organized endeavour in mundane terms. The story very well deserves the treatment that supporters of symbolic interactionism advocate for in organizational studies (e.g. Weick 1995). But, very much in line with a materialist understanding of the pragmatist viewpoint, emphasis is put here on the interaction with and between financial objects proper.

I use the term 'financial object' to refer to any entity that stands as the object of purposeful financial business. One paramount financial object is, of course, what is often referred to as a financial 'product', but can also be termed financial 'instrument' or financial 'service' – or a financial 'security' when one deals with quite standardized, easily fungible products. A financial product is, basically, a contract: a document that states what is sold and bought, by whom and to whom, and which explains, in conditional language, what is going to happen in terms of money transfers. An insurance policy is a good example of a basic form of financial product. A financial 'trade', another type of financial object, is a product viewed from another angle: that of a transaction typically performed between two parties, or 'counterparties' in financial parlance. A product, of course, is designed to be sold, hence traded, but the picture can get quite complex. A product can be traded once, and then traded further when the product is listed on an exchange, but also when it is traded bilaterally in an over-the-counter market. In order to gain a basic understanding of how financial derivatives work, one can imagine an insurance policy that, once bought, can be traded in a secondary market at a fluctuating price. A so-called 'complex' product can imply the existence of multiple trades performed on simpler products with the purpose of generating the revenue or protection that is served under contract to the client and to generate profit for the bank itself. Imagine a product that covers the risk associated with the fluctuation of a number of parameters; selling it also means trading conveniently in the underlying markets in order to make the product stand, or 'hedge' it, as financiers say.

An investment bank accordingly considers each 'trade' and each 'product' by itself, but also as parts of other 'products' and 'trades'. A 'marketplace' (another form of financial object) refers to the circuits through which trades are performed. Such circuits can be more or less institutionally organized spaces in the form of centralized, automated exchanges (including the attendant trading technologies), and OTC (over-the-counter) arrangements in which products are traded bilaterally. In some cases, especially of the latter kind, a fine description of the 'counterparty' (another form of financial object, I would say) is required: its risks, legal characteristics, and accounting entry points. Is a big picture available that would allow all of the financial objects that Thoth Bank engages with to be mapped in a cogent manner? Not quite, to my knowledge (and, I surmise, neither to Thoth Bank's).

Describing financial objects is a concern that becomes explicit in many parts of the organization and outside of it. In the following list, I itemize, quite randomly, sites and situations in which the problem of description can appear inside Thoth Bank: a trader at her desk running a pricing software in order to describe the behaviour of a complex product that has been put on the market; an employee in the marketing department figuring out how to describe a financial product in cogent, pedagogical, but also attractive terms in a brochure; a salesperson talking casually on the phone with an institutional investor in order to roughly describe a trade proposal; an accountant trying to compile several figures in order to describe the overall profit or loss engendered by a financial product over a period of time. Here is another list in which I consider a few comparable situations, but outside the perimeter of the bank: an employee at a regulatory agency describing the functioning and potential risks of a new financial product; a financial engineer trying to describe the hedging parameters of a financial product issued by a competitor; a professor of finance describing a financial product to a group of students in the classroom; a filmmaker critically describing the causes and consequences of a financial service in a documentary film; an employee in a remote retail bank branch describing the pay-off of a financial product to a retail client (you). Note that all of these acts of description can very well refer to the 'same' financial product. The quotation marks, of course, indicate that these descriptions can be – and are in practice – radically different, sometimes consonant but sometimes overtly dissonant. Naturally, it begs the question: are these things really the same? The financial product exhibits referential (one can even dare to say ontological) problems that are similar to the ones identified by Annemarie Mol, for example, in her investigation of the reality of atherosclerosis (Mol 2002). They constitute problematic layers of description which refer to something that, although not overtly fragmented, requires a number of active tactics in order to make it cohere. I conjecture that these tactics are a persistent concern at Thoth Bank; the 'problem of description' was indeed referred to as such, spontaneously, in fieldwork conversations with executive personnel.

The back office and the trouble with finalization

The problem of description is present everywhere. But there are sites within the bank in which it crystallizes in a particularly telling manner. I am referring here, in particular, to the back office. Why the back office? Both back office departments within the bank and clearing and settlement procedures in the marketplace are there precisely to cope with the problem of description in a particularly pressing circumstance: the 'finalization' of financial objects. Financial activity creates bonds.

It opens positions, engages deals and generates exposure. But, at a crucial point in time, obligations are settled, payments are concluded, counterparties are detached, contracts are terminated, assets are transferred and markets are cleared. Finance is, in part, an art of finalization (Millo *et al.* 2005). The vocabulary of sanitation and clarification ('to clear') is an essential part of the financial game. Finance is indeed, perhaps, one of the finest illustrations of the tactics that economic life requires for participants to remain 'quits' after an economic entanglement (Callon 1998; Muniesa 2008a). But this requires work, and participants in the financial services industry often realize that finalization is not always a clear-cut act. There may be a rest – and one can wonder if the residue, the leftover, the subsisting liability is not there to allow for the expression of some sort of a psychoanalytic truth in the conduct of finance. Is there a connection between the gigantic, purposeful money-making machinery of the banking institution and the exacerbation of concern for the traces left behind? What the empirical examination of Thoth Bank reveals, in any case, is that the concern for finalization and its consequences stands almost as the essence of the back office – the banking anus (technically speaking).

In an investment bank, back office and middle office structures support the logistics of operations initiated in the front office departments. The front office is where traders, salespersons and financial engineers work, where the selling and the buying takes place, where products are launched and trades are originated. The middle office is where information about what is being done is compiled and analysed, especially in regard to the activity's translation into monetary terms. The back office is where the engagements are actually served: products are delivered, trades are settled and payments are transferred.

Here is an illustration, quite simplistic, but hopefully pedagogical: a salesperson agrees on the phone to a deal and sells a coverage product to a client who has some kind of exposure. She then tells a trader next to her desk about the deal, and the trader starts executing the trades that will allow the bank to fulfil the terms of the contract and make some money for itself. An employee in the middle office learns about this from the tickets filled in by the salesperson and the trader (which are more or less computerized), inscribes the operations in the bank's books, verifies which links to which, checks market parameters, and reports on profits and losses. Someone in the back office learns about these happenings through similar conduits (also with some sort of computer support), issues confirmations of operations to all involved parties, and sends the relevant signal to the different clearing circuits (directly to the back office departments of the trade counterparty, or through centralized clearing and settlement facilities, depending on the kind of object considered).

The situation I just depicted is simplistic indeed, but one can very well imagine the sort of puzzle that middle office and back office employees can face from time to time. To which contract does this trade correspond? Who changed the account associated with this counterparty? Which indicative prices were used in order to assess the profit estimate for this trade? Where is the last version of the contract and which version was actually sent to the client? What is this payment for? One also must consider the fact that in an organization such as Thoth Bank, there is not one front office but several, not one back office but several, in widely dispersed geographic locations, and operating under several subsidiaries and corporate structures. Of course, Thoth Bank is careful with all that, and this is true most certainly for any investment bank of a comparable size today. Failure to cope swiftly with this script complexity can translate into day-to-day problems, unforeseen charges here and there, and more or less tolerable doses of organizational mess. But it can also translate into traumatic incidents – hence the call for industrious process on the back office side of finance.

Processing descriptions through the banking space

'Industrious process' means organization, and organization today means information systems. Describing financial objects involves talking and writing, but also sorting, computing and transmitting. One of the organizational shibboleths that were heard often at Thoth Bank's headquarters in fieldwork interviews was 'STP', which stands for 'straight through processing'. STP is about streamlining and automating the chain of operations that connects the generation of a trade to its finalization. Here, finance exhibits an essential trait of flux industries: the fluid becomes the leading motive for the organization of production, but also of labour and value (Vatin 1987). But financial objects are not always easily subjected to swift, automated processing, that is, to standardization. Sometimes customization is required. At Thoth Bank, 'customization' was another organizational shibboleth, as was 'exotic', a word often used to refer to products and trades that demanded detailed, 'manual' treatment.

Several back office systems were in use at Thoth Bank at the time of the research (for more technical details, see Muniesa *et al.* 2011). These roughly respected the distinction between the four broad business lines at Thoth Bank: commodities, fixed income, money markets and foreign exchange, and equities and derivatives. But financial objects often cut across these broad categories; derivatives are ubiquitous, composite products, and so-called 'structured' products often include parts from more than one category. The existence and functioning of information systems is the outcome of an organizational, technological and commercial history. Some, for instance, are industry-wide standard systems developed by an information technology vendor. One example of this at Thoth Bank is the system used to process listed options and futures. In terms of problems of description of financial objects, informants indicated that, yes, relying on a standard interface favours the development of shared vocabularies within the industry. But one drawback, some explained, was that the interface sometimes could be slightly at odds with internal organizational terminology. Other back office systems at Thoth Bank were developed in-house. One example was the system for commodities operations. Justification for this was mainly expressed by informants in terms, again, of the description of financial objects: pricing parameters in such an over-the-counter environment are hard to characterize and verify, and operations usually combine a wide range of components (options, futures, currency swaps, fixed income swaps, etc.).

In order to cope with these issues in an elegant and cost-efficient manner, managers at Thoth Bank have developed several templates over the years to make sense of and organize the description and circulation of financial objects within the bank. At the time of the fieldwork, executive managers at Thoth Bank would present the overall back office apparatus in terms of three distinct angles that ought to govern how financial objects are addressed. The first two are the product perspective and the trade perspective. The trade perspective, which is characteristic of middle office processes, focuses on the transaction as the unit of analysis, independent of the types of financial products involved in it. The middle office considers all of the composite elements of a trade initiated by its corresponding front office. The product perspective, which governs back office operations, ignores the individual trade and focuses instead on elementary building blocks which are sorted into homogeneous, specialized categories. The back office handles elements that belong to its speciality (e.g. listed stocks, fixed income, foreign exchange, etc.) and dispatches disparate elements to other dedicated back office systems. A third perspective was also being considered at Thoth Bank as a potential driver for the assessment and reorganization of back office activities: a process perspective. A process perspective focuses on the level of standardization characterizing each specific operation. It distinguishes activities that are suitable for a streamlined treatment from activities that call for a singularized approach. As we can see, all three perspectives are about description. The first two, trade and product, demonstrate the classic difference between a middle office, which focuses on the description of what the front office did (especially in terms of profits and losses), and a back office, which is concerned about finalization and, consequently, the paths taken by different parts of a deal and where they end. The process perspective, however, encapsulates quite well the qualitative aspects of the description of financial objects and of the different styles in which these are written.

Singular objects and written confirmations

'Straight through processing' and 'customization' are two keywords that together define a symptomatic tension within the banking space. Standardization and automation processes affect the description of financial objects and their circulation. But standard and automated are quite demanding states to be in; they require unambiguous algorithmic formulation. Conversely, trades and products that require to be discussed, their terms negotiated, their characteristics explained and their counterparties personally known typically fall into the realm of what economic sociologists have called qualification or singularization (Callon *et al.* 2000, 2002; Karpik 2007, 2010). Here, I am less interested in the fact that financial objects undergo a marketing process (which they do) than in the fact that some demand more emphasis than others in terms of qualitative treatment. Their qualities are surely not formulated from scratch, but they serve novel functions and face multiple calls for explicitness: what does this object do, exactly? How, when, for whom and at what price?

Unsurprisingly, the financial objects that are more exposed to qualitative treatment are the ones that are sold to corporate counterparties. 'Corporate counterparties' are corporate clients such as institutional investors, fund managers or treasury departments in large companies. Managers at Thoth Bank distinguish them from what they refer to as 'interbank counterparties': not clients, but similar banks with whom traders at Thoth Bank interact in order to create the strategies and products developed by the bank. This is what is often alluded to as 'the market'. Let me make it clear that a trade with a corporate counterparty is not something that is accomplished with just one click. Most of the time it involves several face-to-face meetings, signatures, verifications and the prevalence of a technology that epitomizes the conversational form and, hence, the qualitative, singularized description of terms, engagements, purposes and conditions: the telephone (Muniesa 2008b). The other technology that is somewhat pervasive in this area is paper. Texts must be read and signed. Written traces must remain and stand as proof of understanding and engagement. One particular piece of paper insisted upon by informants at Thoth Bank is the trade confirmation. The description of a trade, they said, crystallizes in the confirmation process.

The trade confirmation document plays a decisive role in consolidating the description of the terms, engagements, purposes and conditions of what is about to be done – or, more exactly, what is actually done through the act of printing and relaying that document. The clauses specified in this document protect the bank against legal claims from their clients. Trade confirmation is thus more than a mere validation: it stands as an acknowledged and legally valid definition of the financial product sold to a client. This is particularly true in the case of complex, non-standard products. A back office employee dealing with OTC derivatives at Thoth Bank emphasized the crucial role of this written document in the description process: 'Because we handle a trade that can last for a long period of time, the description of the terms of agreement is essential', he concluded in an interview after describing the meandering process of a complex contract (Muniesa et al. 2011: 1199).

Another employee went on to explain how the confirmation process was generated in the case of a swap treated at the commodities sales desk of Thoth Bank. The trade is handled by a salesperson. As soon as the terms of the trade are agreed upon with the client via telephone, the trade is entered into Thoth Bank's commodities back office system, and the corresponding operations are taken care of by a trader at Thoth Bank who hedges it on the interbank market. The back office system generates confirmations: these are relatively long documents (about four pages) containing the description of the trade, together with legal disclaimers and details based on criteria defined by the International Swaps and Derivatives Association (ISDA). The salesperson validates the document, which is then printed and transmitted to the client. Note that this is actually transmitted by fax – not due to a lack of more modern-day paperless technologies (say, an electronic file), but because the printed nature of this inscriptional device is essential to the process. Only when the document has been printed on paper, dated and signed does it signify the finalization of the description. The terms of disentanglement are then clear, obligations are satisfied and the trade is complete. The quality of the confirmation and the written document associated with it is central in the back office process. A manager in the commodities back office noted, 'The salesperson often brings a confirmation draft when he meets his clients'. Presenting an unsigned confirmation is the equivalent of showing a client what the product looks like.

The role of the confirmation document is not limited to handling the presentation of the financial object to the corporate client. It also plays a crucial role in dismantling a trade, that is, in reducing an operation to its constitutive parts. What the salesperson sells to a corporate counterparty is a composite, packaged product. The description displays information about its ingredients, so to say. Once the trade is engaged, the back office process includes tracking these elementary ingredients. As another employee in the same commodities back office put it, 'the confirmation describes the behaviour of the product'. Thus, the confirmation provides a type of map that indicates what needs to be done in order to make this behaviour happen. The confirmation therefore must summarize the dismantlement process: it indicates directions for the deconstruction of the recipe.

The confirmation does not, however, contain a 'literal' description of this dismantlement process. What does this mean? The content of the confirmation must provide enough flexibility and scope to ensure that the transaction is actionable by the multiple parties involved in the process, but it should not reveal the 'inside' of the product (the informant's words), that is, the financial know-how needed to build and hedge it. The confirmation document is a hybrid document. It stands, first and foremost, as a commercial document that depicts the characteristics of a product in terms of service (coverage, pay-off, etc.), but also as a legal document that defines duties, liabilities, conditions and responsibilities. It also serves as an engineering document that provides instructions for its construction and maintenance, sufficient enough for any party to know what is inside, but not to replicate it (as when one reads the list of ingredients of a dish and, at best, just a summary of the recipe, without details). The confirmation document is the product itself.

The valuation of financial objects as a problem of description

As suggested here and elsewhere, finance is mostly about making money with money. Needless to say, describing financial objects is also (although not only) about describing their value or, in other words, about figuring out how much money is made. Accounting for profits and losses is about counting amounts but also about determining who or what is responsible for them. This process might be considered a front office issue: pricing methods are a constitutive part of the material culture of trading desks. But determining the precise value of a trade is often tackled after things have been done and handled by the departments in charge of finalization, in particular by the middle office and the accounting department.

Several valuation practices exist across the trade and post-trade process at Thoth Bank, confirming one particularly salient observation put forward in the social studies of finance (Beunza and Stark 2004; Stark 2009). This means that the value of an asset, a trade, or a position in the market can be considered through multiple metrics. And I do not mean here that there are several ideas of what things are worth, some being financial and others not, some being economic and others not. I mean that the monetary value of the same financial object can be considered in very different terms by a trader, a salesperson, a back office employee, a risk manager, an accountant or a lawyer, and those terms are not always convergent.

Is this evidence of a flaw in the organization, the bank being unable to secure a univocal principle of valuation? Not quite. Value depends on valuation and valuation is an active, performative process that is meant to serve particular purposes and obey different configurations. This is not to say that value is just subjective, but rather that it is objective in several different ways and from several different angles (Muniesa 2012). Indeed, at Thoth Bank discrepancies between different value metrics can be a problem, and efforts are deployed in order to map them and reduce them to an acceptable, tractable level. In fact, managerial discourse at the time of the fieldwork inside Thoth Bank emphasized the need to introduce homogeneity in valuation practices and to impose a set of common criteria that could be used independently of the object under consideration. Putting things inside a single calculative space is a way of making them manageable (Miller 1994; Callon and Muniesa 2005). And the management of valuation discrepancies is an essential function of post-trade structures in an investment bank.

Discrepancies in the determination of the value of a financial object may often arise, for example, between a front office version of value, and accounting or back office versions of value for the same thing. The front office version, for example, often relies on an immediate estimation of the proverbial 'P&L', the profits and losses generated by an operation, a set of operations, a team at a trading desk, or an individual trader. Fairly enough, this version considers value in terms of economic performance. But some elements, parameters, factors and constraints may be added or modified in other versions. Different from a front office version, although very similar, may be a middle office version that recalculates profits and losses using precise actual market prices, not on-the-spot estimation. In some OTC markets, for example, aggregate price indicators cannot be calculated in real time and need to be reconstructed after the fact. The middle office employee also considers costs that the trader may disregard, such as trading and clearing fees.

But the work does not stop there. The management of valuation discrepancies is handled by middle office P&L departments inside Thoth Bank. A crucial activity there is the assessment and reconciliation of economic results with accounting results. When interviewees attempted to explain the discrepancies between economic results and accounting results at Thoth Bank, they pointed to the need to work with different priorities within specific work practices. They identified two main types of discrepancy – method discrepancies and perimeter discrepancies – which both correspond to classificatory problems identified in the sociology of accounting (Hopwood and Miller 1994; Hatherly *et al.* 2008). What do they mean by 'method discrepancies'? Here is an example: cash lending and borrowing operations are valued using a mark-to-market methodology by the front office, whereas accounting results for these same operations are calculated based on an accrual method in order to conform to domestic regulation. 'Mark-to-market' is the front office-driven way of considering things from a financial viewpoint: the value of an asset is what one can get for it in the market today. But this logic is not all-encompassing within the banking space – at least not at Thoth Bank at the time of the fieldwork. The calculation criteria used to indicate profit varies from one activity to another depending on the objective of the calculation, which is decided by local organizational priorities.

This is the case not only in that particular back office. A similar multiplicity of practices associated with the calculation of value can be found for other financial products. For instance, valuation of operations in money markets at Thoth Bank would be handled at some point following a mark-to-market principle (because these operations are viewed as arbitrage on future positions) and then considered using an accrual method at some other point (because the product is then regarded as a financing tool). To this, add what informants call 'perimeter discrepancies': the way in which the treatment of the product is organized across different front office activity centres (desks), operations units (traders or teams) and books (portfolios, accounts). Even if a common format is shared by front offices and the accounting department, there are elements in the definitions of perimeters that cannot be easily standardized.

Valuation checking is a complex matter that relates not only to discrepancies between front office value criteria and accountancy criteria, but also to other areas. A wide variety of verifications must be performed across different calculative spaces. Checking the coherence of operations within the front office proper is part of this intense activity of verifying the coherence of value descriptions. Reconciling sales orders with trading activities often falls within this type of work. Remember that a complex product that a salesperson sells to a client needs to correspond to the subsequent operations that the trader at Thoth Bank initiates in the interbank market in order to achieve the results envisaged in the product. Middle office and back office departments at Thoth Bank are in charge of verifying this correspondence between operations generated by front office sales desks and operations performed at the front office trading desks. So-called middle office 'ticket processing units' are also responsible for verifying the coherence of pricing parameters. As mentioned above, they must check the prices that have been used in trades against external data. This is particularly relevant in OTC environments where market parameters must be 'manually' gathered from a sample of relevant counterparties. In other words, in order to arrive at 'the' (or rather 'a') value of a trade, multiple choices, verifications and translations must be carried out on several descriptions of value.

Valuation is, in finance as elsewhere, a very constructive process (Muniesa 2012). This does not mean that the process is arbitrary. It is an organized process, supported by sound metrics and conducted by skilled personnel. The process is contingent: it relies on localized certainties, changing purposes and organizational determinations. The process is also solid: value is constructed in the sense that it is industrially constructed. An engineered piece can, of course, fall apart, but this is only proof of the fact that solidity is a difficult state to achieve, a state that demands more construction, and not less. What the back office work at Thoth Bank reveals is the intense maintenance activity that this process requires – maintenance being an aspect of market activities that some anthropologists have not neglected (e.g. Çalışkan 2010). Keep in mind how the performative character of the description of economic things operates in general: these things can be considered as nothing more and nothing less than the accumulation of layers of descriptions. Nothing more, but above all, nothing less, and Thoth Bank is reflexively and explicitly conceived for the organization of layers of descriptions. Do both operational staff and executive managers at Thoth Bank measure the constructivist depth of their work? My opinion is that they do, at least sometimes.

Technocratic mastery and back office intricacy

Thoth Bank in its entirety seems to be preoccupied with the problem of the description of financial objects at several levels. And the locus in which this preoccupation is most vividly conveyed is the back office. Descriptions are multifarious and financial objects are expressed in multiple versions across the entire banking space. But, as we have seen, it is at the site of finalization where these multiple descriptions must cohere and their discrepancies must be addressed. The termination of trades, the clearing of pending obligations, the payment of debts, and the inscription of profits and losses are all tasks that require a *mise à plat* of financial objects: a reasonably clear-cut, indisputable and calculable system of descriptions. This translates into great intricacy as the complexity of financial objects increases. Despite considerable efforts at streamlining, the variety of post-trade organizational arrangements and information systems appears in this respect to be quite irreducible.

Is this intricacy necessary? One could perhaps hope for a simplification of financial activities and for improvement in the general readability of financial objects (e.g. Engelen *et al.* 2011). But that hope is likely to be met with disappointing results. Finance very much partakes of the movement of reflexive modernization that social theorists have identified in the risk-generating effects of risk-mitigation techniques (e.g. Luhmann 1993). Descriptions create angles for the description of descriptions, and the complexity of the overall picture – an incomplete system of descriptions – results from the proliferation of such angles. The amplification of problems of description in the back office departments of investment banks is certainly a companion to the upsurge of interest in the notion of 'operational risk' in financial life (Power 2005, 2007).

'Systemic risk' is another widespread notion that can be traced back to concerns about the accumulation of both complex financial objects and networks of unsettled, pending connections between them: a flaw in one can jeopardize the entire chain of financial entanglements (Aglietta 1995). And observe what happens when measures are taken against these forms of menace. Centralized clearinghouses are often presented as the solution for more security against the odds of OTC markets. Often justified in terms of transparency, these institutional arrangements cancel, to a great extent, the dangers of chain defaults and improve the readability of prices (Millo *et al.* 2005; Grossman *et al.* 2008). But, as soon as a financial object becomes, in effect, more readable and more reliable, financial imagination is unleashed and you can bet that someone will come up with a clever way to turn it into the underlying object of another financial instrument. And the back office must follow.

There is, thus, a quite prosaic way to interpret if not the necessity, at least the likelihood of descriptive intricacy in the financial terrain. This is that complexity creates opportunities for making money. Key traumatic episodes such as the collapse of Barings Bank have been partially interpreted in terms of control of information systems and back office tinkering (Drummond 2003; Brown 2005; Greener 2006; Abraham and Sardais 2008). Part of Nick Leeson's activities centred on strategies of camouflage in the description of operations. Back office intricacy was also crucial in similarly notable cases, for instance in the 2008 trading loss incident at Société Générale prompted by the actions of Jérôme Kerviel (Krawiec 2009; Moodie 2009; Previtali 2009). True, these two episodes were about financial losses. But the purpose in both cases was to make money through the ingenious mastery of back office arrangements. Note in this respect that, most famously, it was after a career in these areas that Jérôme Kerviel was invited to exercise his talents in the front office.

The crux of the Kerviel affair was a matter of unfavourable, unsettled positions that were described as standing profits through the skilful use of back office technicalities. It should be noted that Société Générale was at that time justifiably well known for its conscientious and diligent approach to the subject matter. What happened with Kerviel could have happened elsewhere – it actually happens all the time, but the losses are usually not important enough to make a fuss. And sometimes, of course, there are profits, not losses – but we do not hear about that in the news.

But, if the surge in the description of financial objects is a crucial element of contemporary evolutions in the financial services industry, then what does this tell us about the power of description? Complexity, intricacy, sophistication and diversity can be said to significantly hamper an even distribution in the power of description. Standardization and streamlining may be understood as part of a trend toward simplification but also, perhaps more convincingly, as the vehicles for a sharper separation between, on the one hand, the engineering and appropriation of financial objects and, on the other hand, their operational manipulation. Efforts to cope with the intricacy of financial objects foster an explicit concern for description at the back office level. The well-known fact that back office services usually follow a front office drive is, in a sense, partly balanced (or at least accompanied) by the emergence of novel types of computational, organizational and technocratic capacities based on the mastery of back office arrangements.

4 Discovering stock prices

One of the most precious treasures of the modern naturalist style of economic reasoning is the expression 'price discovery'. That is the way economists and educated practitioners talk about how trading prices are attained in stock exchanges and other organized markets for tradable products. There is some market truth to be achieved (the word 'truth' has indeed some currency in the literature that analyses these processes from an economic vantage point), and this is the potential price that ought to clear transactions in the most equilibrated and justified manner. But sometimes things get messy, as the saying goes, and this potential price is not attained in real trading practice. So, efforts must be made in order to develop the interfaces that allow for a collective discovery of that price.

Is there a problem? Well, yes. In reality, stock prices are not discovered. They are made, they are fabricated. They are artefacts which are immanent to trading practice and to the exchange architecture within which trading takes place. So-called 'price discovery' is, as a matter of fact, an object of tinkering, an object of engineering in the most sophisticated cases. Since the advent of telecommunication technologies and then of computer technologies within the stock exchange, the quality of price formation has been taken care of through algorithmic configurations that compete in a harsh market for market technologies. In this chapter, I use materials gathered from 1999 to 2002 on exchange automation in financial markets, already exploited in a few publications on the case of the Arizona Stock Exchange (Muniesa 2011a) and on the case of the Paris Bourse (Muniesa 2000a, 2000b, 2005, 2007). As we will see, apart from reiterating the fact that prices are performed (which is of course true, but this is a truth that is today widely acknowledged in the social studies of finance), there again exist quite interesting elements that can facilitate refinement of the problems of performativity that I have signalled in the preceding pages.

Making market perfection algorithmically explicit

The fact that the ideals of market equilibrium established in classical and neoclassical economics are not very explicit about how this equilibrium is attained is widely acknowledged today. Of course, the classics told us about some sort of a process – for example, collective groping in an abstract auction, most famously posited by Léon Walras – but this did not include precise instructions for successful implementation (Teira Serrano 2001). How should agents be prevented from trading at 'false' prices, whatever this means? And what should be done if more than one 'true' price is found?

Those questions call for a somewhat algorithmic formulation of the course of action. 'If ... then ... go to ... terminate'. And this is precisely what economics has become, to a quite great extent, in the wake of the 'machine turn' that characterized specialities such as experimental economics, operations research, mechanism design, auction theory and market microstructure (see Izquierdo Martín 1996; Mirowski 1996, 2002, 2007; Guala 2005). The tricky thing (which is quite interesting from the angle of performativity) is that the algorithmic formulation of price creation was also, from the 1970s onwards, the task undertaken by those who were in charge of producing these prices: the consultants, engineers and economists working for stock exchanges, brokerage houses and investment firms. 'Price discovery automation' – a wave of electronic interventions that characterized financial markets all over the world and which culminated, sometimes quite resoundingly, with the abolition of open-outcry and face-to-face trading – was presented as both a unique contribution to the purification of price formation (i.e. the removal of the barriers that prevented the expression of the market in the form of truly transparent prices) and a blatant demonstration of the fact that price formation is a technological service (i.e. something that does not happen in and by itself, something explicitly manufactured, utterly unnatural).

In the 1980s and the 1990s, the North American organized financial markets were the scene of innumerable initiatives for computer-assisted liquidity enhancement (i.e. enabling more trading), ranging from proposals for a consolidated electronic national stock market system to plans to create competing electronic trading venues (Lee 1998). They all raised issues of relevance and regulation, of feasibility and opportunity, generating passions and contestations. They challenged the very definition of what an 'exchange' was supposed to be. They introduced into market regulatory parlance words that better described computer technologies than commercial transactions (i.e. 'system', 'data', 'access', 'execution', 'program', 'network'). They activated circumstantial (but crucially performative) associations between financiers, technologists and economists in the emerging business for market technologies (Muniesa 2011a).

The case of the so-called Arizona Stock Exchange, although exotic, is notable in this regard. That was the name adopted in 1992 by Wunsch Auction System, Inc., a proprietary trading system imagined by Steven Wunsch in the late 1980s in New York, which was based on the trading practice that Wunsch and his colleagues had developed at the derivatives department of Kidder, Peabody & Co., an investment and brokerage house. That practice, known as 'sunshine trading', consisted in increasing the concentration of liquidity at a point in time by publicly announcing that they would be ready to sell this or that at a predefined moment, hence 'calling' the market. The Wunsch Auction System rendered this idea through an electronic call auction: an auction that, instead of running continuously over time with bids and asks popping up and getting executed against what was available at that moment, would concentrate the matching of buy and sell orders at a discrete moment in time, hence favouring the accumulation of demand and supply. The prices served by the system were supposed to be (and were indeed to a great extent) more stable, more relevant and definitely cheaper to obtain that the ones produced by institutional trading venues such as the New York Stock Exchange.

An encounter with Vernon Smith and other experimental economists academically sanctioned the call auction device, and happened to motivate the system's move from New York to Phoenix, Arizona (Friedman and Rust 1993; Smith 1994). The Arizona Corporation Commission had approached Smith's laboratory at the University of Arizona to seek electronic inspiration for the establishment of a local stock exchange, and was redirected by the scientist to Wunsch's commercial version of the mechanism that they were demonstrating in the experimental setting. 'Academic theories tested heretofore only in the laboratory are no longer merely academic', as Wunsch himself nicely put in the promotional (and, we agree, simplistic) endorsement printed on the back cover of a book edited by Daniel Friedman and John Rust on auction models and experiments (Friedman and Rust 1993). The Arizona Stock Exchange turned into an archetypal character in the market design literature that presented the electronic call action as the device that could instate orderly and sound price discovery in North American financial markets, and in markets all over the world (Schwartz 2001; Schwartz *et al.* 2003). It sided there with another unavoidable model: the electronic call auction used at the Paris Bourse to open and close the trading session (Muniesa 2000a, 2000b, 2007).

Why is this of interest? I want to focus here on one of the problems of performativity that these kinds of realities exacerbate: the problem of explicitness. Let us start with a classic, though problematic, statement: the best price (the most perfect, most equilibrated, optimal price, the price that contains more being at the lowest expense, to put it as Leibniz would have) is the one that corresponds to the single point at which supply and demand schedules intersect; that is, the single point at which the most buy and sell orders can clear in the most compatible and satisfactory manner. The single point is, as almost everybody knows, to be found by the proverbial invisible hand (Ingrao and Israel 1987, 1990). Or, in other terms, by the imaginary, anonymous and fictitious, though necessary, mediator that clears the market on behalf of participants: the legendary Walrasian auctioneer, the $n+1$ player that allows all the other players to coexist in mutual indifference, through the peaceful expression of prices, as lucidly remarked by Jean-Pierre Dupuy (1992a: 50).

One problem is that this point, formulated by the proverbial economist, is hard to find in reality. A classical economist noted, 'We know what economists mean by market: not a concrete site where purchase and sale are carried out, but a space in which parties are connected through relations of free commerce and in which prices are adjusted easily and promptly' (Cournot 1838: 55, my translation). Another classical economist would confirm that this happens in a 'hypothetical regime' and that the market upon which the rational (as opposed to experimental) method of pure political economy operates is 'ideal' (Walras 1926: xi). The problem is that markets exist in places that do not prove hospitable for the advent of this 'single point'. Yes, sometimes markets have formed in particular venues with the explicit purpose of finding and displaying this 'single point', and the classics have often looked to the stock exchange for an empirical correlate of their abstracted space. For instance, Walras was reportedly inspired by the Paris Bourse of his time. However, recent reports seem to show that this inspiration was not very accurate (Kregel 1995; Walker 2001).

We meet here the preferred line of the economic sociologist: markets are not as Walras posits them. There is no Walrasian auctioneer in reality. Markets are socially embedded – embedded in interpersonal networks, geographical territories and physical spaces, in social institutions, political structures and cultural forms. Only a nineteenth-century economist would dare to disembed them in order to restore the 'single point' that the rational method of pure political economy requires. Those were precisely the nineteenth-century 'academic incantations' that Karl Polanyi famously identified as the intellectual front of disembedding that led to the destruction of civilization in Europe (Polanyi 1944).

Let me be clear: I do not think that disembedding a market here and there should always be interpreted as a menace to humanity. Polanyi's was an historically motivated view, not an assessment of the dangers of trading things at a 'single point', and his concern was more on the type of competitive markets that developed for land, labour and money. But he is credited with having suggested the idea of 'embeddedness' as a weapon against a formalistic, economistic, neoclassical view of markets. Mark Granovetter's middle-range version of the notion (embeddedness is about the embeddedness of commercial transactions into interpersonal networks of mutual recognition) has prompted a productive stream of research which has contributed, insistently, to the understanding of the functioning (even the economic functioning) of markets that do not quite resemble the ideal of the 'single point' (e.g. Granovetter 1985).

But what happens when an engineer purposefully builds a market that resembles that ideal? Marie-France Garcia's important study of the economic engineering of a wholesale agricultural exchange for strawberries at Fontaines-en-Sologne has brought to economic sociology the ultimate demonstration of the material processes at work in the embedding of a market into a neoclassical 'price discovery' doctrine (Garcia 1986; Garcia-Parpet 2007). Garcia did not focus specifically on the problem of explicitness. Rather, she was interested in the power struggles between strawberry growers and wholesale dealers and in the fate of local market life. But, through her analysis of the minute details of the implementation of a so-called perfect, transparent market, she described what one could very well call a trial of explicitness.

The economic consultant who led the construction of the new market warehouse and the new electronic auction mechanism so as to have supply and demand schedules meet at a single point (through price, and definitely not through interpersonal relations) did not rely on a turnkey solution. His neoclassical intuition was pretty much that – an intuition. In order to have a sound market price, we should start gathering buyers and sellers into a single point, making them express their willingness to buy or to sell only through the public display of prices. But how? What kind of auction? An ascending-price auction, or a descending-price auction? With buyers and sellers in the same room, or in different rooms? With telephones, or without? With an option for a second round if no price is found, or not? All of the practical details of the device were put to the test of adjustments and refinements so as to prevent 'bad' prices from emerging, but those adjustments and refinements were also calls for a clearer, more explicit understanding of what a 'good' and a 'bad' price ought to be. This performative process of empirical clarification closely resembles the one described by Francesco Guala in his foundational study of the economically inspired construction of spectrum auctions in the United States (Guala 2001).

Putting market equilibrium to the test of detailed explication is a matter of imagining and implementing rules, of coding that corresponds quite nicely to what Laurent Thévenot once called 'investments in forms' (Thévenot 1984). In the wake of the 'machine turn' in market design, it becomes also a matter of algorithmic formulation and actual computer programming. As famously pointed out by Donald Knuth, the algorithm, compared to a stated rule, instruction or recipe, introduces two quite demanding features: the elimination of vagueness and the necessity of termination (Knuth 1977). The possibility of being executed by a machine too, of course, but that seems secondary. What counts is radical explicitness. All situations are to be considered and all possible courses of action solved unambiguously in a finite (and preferably elegant) number of steps. No 'We will deal with that when the situation arises'; no 'It depends on how you interpret it'. All possibilities will be contemplated, all combinations will be exhausted. An algorithm is indeed exhausting in a sense not dissimilar from the one Gilles Deleuze spotted in the combinatorial procedures for (desolate) optimization in Samuel Beckett's characters (Deleuze 1992, 1995).

The same goes for markets. The algorithmic formulation of price discovery does not escape that rule. You ought to define a neatly predefined typology of orders: buy and sell orders, but also orders with or without price limits, orders with or without hidden volumes, orders with or without specific priorities, orders with or without special conditional clauses, and so on. And then you ought to define the rules of interaction between these orders: you match them in a certain order and according to specific priorities; you match them at specific prices among several possible matches; you display the generated files under certain conditions, and so on. No 'Forget about first in, first out for a moment'; no 'Well, let's just split it between the two'; no 'Sorry, let's try that again'. As I indicated earlier, from the 1980s onward, price discovery in financial markets became an intense field of algorithmic creativity, sometimes purely conjectural, sometimes deeply industrial. 'Price discovery automation' became the name of a game which implied careful coding of the rules governing the determination of prices, and an equally careful exhaustion of possible states. This became a hot topic, and an entire competitive, sometimes bitter, market developed for these liquidity-enhancing technologies. But when you look at the text of these algorithms, you can very well think of Beckett's instructions for his television play *Quad* (how to clear all possible options for walking around and across a square stage in finite, indifferent patterns).

So what brought algorithmic formulation to the elliptical 'single point' of sound price discovery? Did the cold algorithmic plot get a univocal ending? Did market computational designers flesh out the neoclassical fantasy and come up with the ultimate 'single point' procedure? Which mechanism won the explicitness contest? What is the true price and which is the mechanical path that leads to it? Was the call auction at the Arizona Stock Exchange the thing? Or was it another one? The Paris Bourse, perhaps the electronic version? Answers to these questions are rather disappointing to anyone who would actually believe in the neoclassical promise. No single, pure, univocal solution sprang from that algorithmic frenzy. There was no winner, no ultimate mechanism. On the contrary, what the trial of explicitness originated was the proliferation of a wide variety of algorithmic configurations, each solving a few problems but generating new, unforeseen ones. Types of auction mechanisms and orders, and conditions of execution and allocation intermingled together into a rather competitive market for market computer solutions, all with their own pros and cons, contributions to previous problems and problematic externalities.

This is easy to understand for anyone who has had the opportunity to experience what a 'computer solution' is in practice: a chain of further problems, a cascade of updates, an endless interplay of framing and overflowing. The same goes for markets. Some notable epistemologists of economics have even toyed with the idea of considering markets in terms of an evolutionary proliferation of algorithmic forms, an ecology of 'evolving computational entities' as Philip Mirowski put it, in association with a co-author who, it seems, ended up well positioned in the profitable world of algorithmic trading, which amounts to arbitraging that ecology (Mirowski and Somefun 1998).

The Arizona Stock Exchange was a tiny step in a gigantic trial of explicitness that began in the 1970s as a quest to figure out how to converge all buy and sell orders to a 'single point'. Fischer Black made a seminal contribution, focused on how to get rid of intermediaries in the stock exchange (in particular, 'specialists' at the New York Stock Exchange) through a double-auction electronic mechanism (Black 1971a, 1971b). The idea of a continuous double auction began to populate the specialized literature (e.g. Domowitz 1990, 1992, 1993). And this literature soon began to cite numerous field examples. Among the most relevant was CATS, the Computer Assisted Trading System developed in the 1970s for the Toronto Stock Exchange that served as basis for CAC, Cotation Assistée en Continu, the electronic trading system that replaced the open-outcry market at the Paris Bourse in the late 1980s (Muniesa 2005; Majury 2007). Continuous time brought advantages to price discovery processes: a double-auction algorithm could generate matching prices as orders would hit the market (i.e. the central memory of the server), dispatching them according to a set of priority rules and transmitting the resulting prices in real time back to the market (i.e. the remote computer clients of the client-server architecture). But the continuous auction was a solution that generated new problems. In a number of situations, prices produced by the architecture became too volatile, not representative, and not sufficiently meaningful (Muniesa 2007).

The 'electronic call auction' then emerged as one possible next step in the conquest of the 'single point': buy and sell orders should concentrate into a single point in space, but also into a single point in time, so as to prevent fragmentation of price discovery. Advocates of the Arizona Stock Exchange found in economics an elegant source of justification – Maurice Allais, for example, was quoted in the exchange's newsletter calling continuous trading an 'aberration' (Muniesa 2011a: 9). In Paris, the market engineers in charge of developing a comparable technology for the determination of closing prices (the '*fixing de clôture*' was an electronic call auction designed to increase the representativeness of prices produced at the end of the trading session) also referred to some classical economists, including Walras. However, as a manager at the Paris Bourse put it in a fieldwork interview, 'Walras did not go as far as us in the details' (Muniesa 2007: 389). What a pleasant rendering of what an algorithmic trial of explicitness is.

And the game did not stop there, of course, as the electronic call auction demanded more and more explicitness, and more solutions to problems arising from solutions to previous problems. During a call auction, the memory of the system is open for incoming buy and sell orders. But these are not executed as they arrive, they are just accumulated. After a while, the memory is closed and an algorithm calculates the price that best clears the stored orders. But 'best clears' is open to interpretation. It is unusual that, at a given price, exactly all the buy and sell orders that are compatible with that price (equal or higher for sell orders, equal or lower for buy orders) will be served. So which price should be used? Well, perhaps precisely the one that leaves fewer orders unexecuted. But, again, several prices can meet that criteria and a decision must be programmed.

Market engineers in Phoenix, Paris and elsewhere needed to come up with an algorithmic plot that would justify, quite circumstantially, the solution finally developed (e.g. take the average among compatible prices, take the price that differs the least from the price obtained in the last auction, etc.). And what happens with the surplus buy or sell orders that matched that price but that nevertheless could not be served because of lack of volume? Again, the composition of an algorithmic principle for allocation needed to be carefully envisaged. And plain time priority (i.e. 'first in, first out') was far from being the sole and the simplest solution in Paris or Phoenix; the early CAC algorithm at the Paris Bourse used a 'roundtable' allocation principle, and the Arizona Stock Exchange developed several combinations of price priority and time priority. And all these questions arose in the first place because it was decided that a call auction price was preferred to a continuous auction price. But what if the desired artefact is precisely a price that varies perceptibly over time, a price that has some kind of continuous volatility? In that case, other algorithms, other protocols, other directions for explicitness, other instances of the 'single point' are in order.

Potential, real, virtual and actual prices

A price discovery algorithm is a designation apparatus. One can easily see how well the notion of collective assemblage of enunciation (*agencement collectif d'énonciation*, in French) developed by Félix Guattari and Gilles Deleuze fits this machinery (Deleuze and Guattari 1980, 1987; Guattari 2011). A price discovery algorithm indeed enunciates. It produces signs that signify what the market is meant to say. We call those signs prices (Muniesa 2007). Market engineers who are working out the 'single point' mechanism are field semiotic engineers: they care for the representativeness of the signs they produce, their readability, their success. Their particular blend of semiotics is of the pragmatist kind, indeed. The 'single point' must be worked out, and what we learn from the recent history of this working out is that it is intensively performative. It is when one attempts to 'discover', 'unveil' and 'decipher' the hidden position of the 'single point' that one discovers that there are actually myriad possible points, and that their rationale and justification, their existence and behaviour, will depend exactly on the technological efforts that one has to make in order to provoke them.

One telling result of the upsurge of price discovery technologies is the phenomenal augmentation of the quantity of prices. If you count prices as empirical events, I am willing to bet (and this is just an informed prediction since there is no practical way to actually count them) that there are significantly more now than there were before the development of stock exchange automation and electronic trading in the 1980s. New, resoundingly profitable and hazardous practices such as algorithmic trading and high-frequency trading today are based precisely on the quantitative exploitation of an overcrowded flow of prices (Lenglet 2011; MacKenzie *et al.* 2012). The collective assemblage of enunciation has definitely added to this flow.

It is perhaps now time, in the light of all this, to address the problem of the virtuality of prices. It is clear from the quite naturalizing vernacular of 'price discovery' that there is a sense in which there would be prices that are not quite real (not attained in reality), but are potential: they are there, ideated, ready to come into being if the conditions of expression (or of discovery) are given. Professional philosophers would probably dislike my express rendering of the problem here, but I nonetheless think it is useful. This idea of potential price calls for a rather linear understanding of the link (of similarity and dissimilarity, of felicitous or infelicitous *adequatio*) between what is going on and what could be going on in optimal circumstances, that is, ideally. An alternative is needed to this linear view, I claim, one that sees in the process of explication a radically creative, constructive, performative process.

Following Henri Bergson, in Gilles Deleuze's version, one can suggest an alternative to the relationship between the potential and the real, which is to shift attention to the relationship between the virtual and the actual (Deleuze 1988b, 1994). Something virtual, a virtual price for example, would be something real, in a sense, something living in a particular place, or in many (perhaps only in the mind of Léon Walras, although this was a very real mind), or perhaps in none particularly, but that can be actualized in another place. And the terms of this displacement (it is, literally, about changing place) are not the repetition, the immutability, the adequacy or the conservation of shape and features. The terms are the multiplicity, the transformation, the opportunity and the generation of occasions. Actualization is enactment, and not all acts look alike. But enactment is enrichment of the virtual, not impoverishment. Power (*potentia*), if any, is on the side of the act. Actualization, or explication for that matter, is the motor. The virtual is what is left behind. It is the shred (it is definitely incomplete) that seeks in the actual something to refer to (Noël 2007). But it is the actual that leads the referential process. The virtual is realized, not in the sense of implementation of the prefigured, not even in the sense of accomplishment of the wanted, but rather in the sense of fathoming, gauging, penetrating what happens, what might happen or what ought to happen. And this of course takes place in multiple, often conflicting manners.

The designation apparatuses known today in economic circles as price discovery mechanisms are not there to turn real the potential of the 'single point' fantasy. Their job is to conduct the work of actualization that situates a virtual configuration in a specific site of explication (an algorithmic configuration, as it happens). This claim is less the consequence of a philosophical standpoint than the result of candid observation of the referential ventures that translated into the proliferation of countless 'single points' in the financial landscape.

It is interesting to remark in this respect that the very dreams of automation that used the 'single point' optimality argument as a means of fostering a race for the computational manufacturing of prices ended up being at the origin of the current business of exploiting, precisely, the lack of the single point. I'm referring to high-frequency trading and algorithmic trading: practices that aim at capturing revenue from the minute discrepancies that can exist between several price discovery processes, including microscopic discrepancies between the spatial and temporal locations of orders on the electronic paths to the execution site (Lenglet 2011; MacKenzie *et al.* 2012). Even today, these practices are sometimes justified as a nice contribution to the unintended consolidation of liquidity, that is, to the production of the optimal single point. But this is just another instalment of the good old tale of private vices turning into public virtues, in cybernetic guise (Hayek 1945). Honestly, I still cannot see a single point emerging. But I see the proliferation of actual prices that lead the referential escalation.

The trouble with second-order transparency

'Transparency' – I should apologize for not having insisted so far on this crucial keyword in the justification of price discovery automation and electronic trading. A glance at the use of this word in recent economic literature provides, first, a strong quantitative impression (it is everywhere) and, second, a disconcerting sense of ambiguity (see Grossman *et al.* 2008). And this is particularly the case in literature specialized in the production of prices in financial markets. The promise of transparency is deeply connected to the problem of embeddedness that economic sociologists have emphasized in their understanding of the formation of markets. Is a market in which people operate bilaterally through interpersonal networks of mutual recognition transparent? Or is that rather opaque in comparison to a market in which trades are formed through the public display of prices with no private interaction? But is a transparent market then a market in which people do not see each other? It is a bizarre idea, though fully compatible with the polysemy of a notion that always requires qualification.

In their influential examination of transparency in architecture, Colin Rowe and Robert Slutzky attempted to identify two rather opposite perspectives: one perspective relies on a literal understanding of the capacity of seeing things in their depth through a translucent medium, while the other focuses on an idea of frontal presentation of things in an abstracted space that allows their functions, rather than their depth, to be seen systematically (Rowe and Slutsky 1963). The contrast between Walter Gropius and Le Corbusier in the articulation of transparency would follow that path, for example. But the contrast between, on one hand, a face-to-face trading institution or an over-the-counter arrangement (where you see who you are dealing with) and, on the other hand, a centralized, public electronic platform (where you see price expressions frontally) follows that path too, in my view.

It is true, though, that transparency in financial markets today tends to imply the second meaning: transparency through the display of prices rather than through interpersonal recognition. Note that calls for more transparent markets usually translate into an explicit critique of OTC markets (i.e. trades done bilaterally, over-the-counter, typically on the telephone between two individuals who know each other) and the defence of centralized clearing mechanisms (i.e. computational institutions that stand as a single third party to every trade and guarantee a sound, anonymous matching process). Transparency means anonymity. This understanding of transparency may sound counter-intuitive if considered from a literal vantage point. The transparency-making device prevents you from seeing directly who you are trading with, making that irrelevant. It is also counter-intuitive if considered from the angle of face-to-face interaction, an angle notoriously reclaimed by a sociological understanding of sense-making in the market. You lose the insight gained from watching people and you must cope with a faceless representative of the market – namely, the screen (a notion which can convey, paradoxically enough, both an idea of displaying or broadcasting and an idea of partitioning or concealing).

I would like to call that type of transparency second-order transparency. This is an overt reference to the cybernetic tradition, a tradition that, obviously, was there sitting in the front row in the intellectual and technical developments that fed the 'machine turn' in economics and operations research from the 1940s onwards (Mirowski 2002). 'Second-order observation' was among the shibboleths of the reflexive wave in cybernetic developments prompted by authors such as Heinz von Foerster, Gordon Pask or Francisco Varela (e.g. von Foerster 2003). That was a wave that Niklas Luhmann swiftly translated into his monumental theory of social systems; in short, a society is a system in which units are observations, and second-order observations constitute systems that observe that system of first-order observations from one particular angle. However, to my knowledge, the social scientist who most radically entered the guts of the original second-order cybernetic intelligence was possibly Jesús Ibáñez (see Ibáñez 1985, 1990, 1991).

The idea of second-order transparency and its rationale for understanding the things examined here can perhaps be derived from what Jean-Pierre Dupuy, a fine analyst of cybernetic reason (Dupuy 1994, translated as Dupuy 2000), has called 'von Foerster's conjecture' (Dupuy 1982, 1992b: 255–62; Koppel *et al.* 1987; see also Ibáñez 1990; Izquierdo Martín 1996). Take a system of related mutual observations between agents (say, a market), and take a second-order observer that is making sense of the system from a particular angle (say, an economist, looking at it from the angle of aggregate prices). In Dupuy's rendering, the conjecture is that the richer and more complex first-order observations are, the more sense the system will make for observers inside it, but the less sense it will make for an external, second-order observer. Conversely, if the rules governing observation among agents are trivial, agents will be alienated since they will not recognize themselves in the aggregated outcome of their actions, but the system will make sense to an external observer. A system in which members recognize themselves is transparent to them since they situate themselves, artificially, in a position of exteriority that we usually call 'society', but opaque to a second-order observer who finds it messy. A system that prioritizes second-order transparency requires trivial rules, and is therefore somewhat opaque (putting sense out of reach) for internal participants. But, in contrast, it provides a neat delineation of behaviour and rationale from the second-order angle.

Dupuy was explicitly thinking about markets, particularly classical and neoclassical kinds, when he formulated this conjecture, which was reportedly based on a legendary (and obviously fantastic) conversation with Heinz von Foerster hosted by Ivan Illich in Cuernavaca, México, in January 1976 (Dupuy 1982: 11–28). For Dupuy, von Foerster's cybernetic intuition was a key to understanding the process that leads to the schematic constitution of society, that is, the 'exteriorization of the social being' in Dupuy's terms, and the problem of alienation that this process often carries, that is, members not recognizing this exteriority as an outcome of their activities.

Market prices constitute a fine laboratory for understanding the rules that govern this process of 'auto-transcendence', again in Dupuy's terms. Once in a while, sociologists of financial markets note an intriguing contrast in the vocabulary of the market put forward by market participants: a participant will reclaim authorship on the market, seeing in a price the outcome of her own intervention, but then another one will talk about the market price as a transcendent statement, something exterior to her (e.g. Brügger 2000: 236–40; see also Muniesa 2007). Dupuy's terms are, once again, of help: the 'exteriorization of an endogenous fixed point' is the production of a point of recognition (e.g. a single price at a single point) that aggregates collective action and that is indeed produced by that collective action, but that transcends this production process and stands as the outcome of an aggregate being that we sometimes call 'the market', without being totally sure that this could mean 'us'. And this effect of otherness is what Dupuy aptly called alienation. Economic sociologists of Polanyian obedience would perhaps prefer to call it disembeddedness. And I think anyone can recognize here the idea of 'society' that economically oriented behavioural scientists usually defend (i.e. little dots estranged in a traffic jam or in a speculative bubble).

The material culture of financial markets is a culture of second-order transparency, at least for financial markets of the electronic, automated, centralized kind. This does not cover the entire financial landscape, of course. Keep in mind that considerable chunks of financial activities are done in OTC (over-the-counter) markets where transactions are bilateral and deeply embedded in social networks. But transparency in financial markets today is definitely interpreted in terms of second-order transparency. Price discovery automation, an adventure whose intellectual angle was explicitly informed by the conquest of the optimal 'single point', ended up producing an informational environment that would serve the requirements of a second-order observer (the king economist, the market engineer), trivializing the procedures governing transactions. Making observations meaningful meant participants (but only the properly equipped ones) switching to second-order observation, which is pretty much what happened. Price discovery automation pretty much led to the escalation in technologies of price meta-observation that turned traders into assemblages of reflexive quantitative gear (Beunza and Stark 2012; MacKenzie *et al.* 2012). The trouble is that what we are now left with is an overcrowded, saturated mass of externalities, blind spots and cracks whose dangers no aggregative magic is likely to cancel. Curbing escalation in price discovery would rather mean restoring parsimony to that discovery process, thickening it up more, rarefying the occasions in which the price of financial things ought to be determined. But that, of course, would mean losing business (escalation means business).

Provoking prices of particular kinds

Stock prices are performative achievements. Market technologies produce prices, and this applies to algorithmic configurations as much as to the conversational configurations characteristic of the speech acts of face-to-face negotiation (Preda 2001, 2003, 2006, 2009). But to say that prices are performative achievements is not very helpful. Yes, they are. So what? What is interesting is to ask what kinds of prices one gets from this or that type of performance. Alex Preda's investigation of the meanders and effects of the diffusion of the stock ticker in financial markets illustrates a shift in price qualities quite well (Preda 2003, 2006). The formation of prices on the floor of the New York Stock Exchange or the Paris Bouse in the nineteenth century was a series of interactional events: speech acts (e.g. 'I take'), augmented by a written trace (e.g. tickets) that would keep track of the interactional nature of such events, stating and certifying who bought or sold to whom, when and for how much. The stock ticker, a telegraphic transmission technology that allowed quoted prices to be communicated at a distance

76 *Elementary case studies*

(the 'ticker tape' is the continuous paper strip on which a stock name, price and volume were printed), transformed these semantic qualities of prices. These indeed progressively approached the shape that most of us associate today with the idea of stock prices: a continuous flow of anonymous prices, naturally represented in the form of charts. The ticker tape provoked, or at least magnified, a number of characteristics of prices that became central to understanding what observing them was about. It fostered the possibility of arbitrage, stimulated chart analysis and, last but not least, contributed to the development of a financial culture for which looking at financial objects meant, first and foremost, looking at the tape (which was certainly not the case beforehand).

What kinds of prices were prompted by the technologies examined here? Which qualities did price discovery automation end up granting them? Two syndromes are worth highlighting here beyond the obvious observation that such configurations produce anonymous, disembedded, estranged prices which nonetheless might live up to criteria of economic optimality. These two syndromes are intertwined and govern what I claim is a radical transformation in the nature and function of prices in finance. Price discovery automation was probably not the only factor behind them, but it helped consistently. The first of such syndromes is the uncommercial condition of prices and the second is their substrate function. What does this mean, exactly?

Prices produced in a centralized electronic trading environment go well beyond the principle of the commercial transaction. They even circumvent the very idea of trading. How is this so? A commercial transaction derives, in principle, from a situation in which trading parties express willingness to sell or purchase a determined object and meet at the trading venue with the explicit purpose of agreeing on a price and settling a transaction. Automating the so-called price discovery process might have been presented, in the early days, as a way to enhance the possibility of attaining sound prices in an overcrowded venue, by simultaneously solving the problems of finding a concurring party for a trade and the problem of calculating the price that most optimally would clear pending bids and asks (i.e. aggregating all to a single point). But the fact is that price discovery automation produced, above all, a medium for the rapid, automatic production of prices, irrespective of their commercial purpose. To want to buy or sell a determined quantity of stock shares might be fairly common motives for putting an order through the electronic system, but definitely not the only ones, and perhaps not the most common ones nowadays.

A trader may just need to get a particular price at the end of the Paris Bourse trading session because this end-of-the-day price is used as a reference to assess her trading performance, or because that figure is used to calculate the value of something else. She does not bother expressing any willingness to buy or to sell but instead uses a program to send an automatic volley of orders in the direction determined by the program at the time determined by the program (Muniesa 2007).

Some macro programming in a spreadsheet application can accomplish such a task, and this form of automated trading was widespread in the 1980s and 1990s. Consider for example how program trading (the automated transmission of batches of orders) came to the forefront of interpretations of the cascade of circumstances that translated into the October 1987 stock market crash (see MacKenzie 2004). Things got more sophisticated in the 2000s, as more sophisticated software developments coupled with advanced hardware (i.e. faster machines, better wires) opened up newer repertoires of market intervention that were even more remarkably at odds with the idea of wanting to buy this stock or wanting to sell that other one. You do not care about buying or selling this or that, you are just in the business of arbitraging infinitesimal variations in the global compound of price discovery nodes. This is what algorithmic trading and high-frequency trading are about, with an emphasis on the automation of the trading decision for the first and on the exploitation of physical transmission conditions for the second. Today, interpreting a stock market chart in terms of sellers meeting buyers is outdated at best, absurd at worst. Prices still stand for the intersection of something, but this is the intersection of 'price-fixing signals', I prefer to say, rather than of 'supply' and 'demand'. They are surely not standing for the transcription of what one would readily call commercial transactions.

In fact (and this leads to the second syndrome of the qualities of automatically discovered prices) stock prices today serve less as vehicles for the commerce of capital stock than as some sort of merchandise in and of itself; that is, as a product that provides the raw material for further business. The commercial purpose of the immense quantities of prices produced by the automated stock exchange is to provide the stuff ('underlying' prices) that serves as a substrate for all kinds of derivative financial activities. The idea that derivative finance emerges on top of plain finance as an overarching probabilistic technique for assessing, insuring and hedging an underlying reality is quite *passé*. Rather, it is the other way around: first comes derivative finance, and then matter is produced that can serve as its substrate (see Ayache 2010).

And it is true that the commercial rationale for 'liquidity enhancement' and 'price improvement' that governed the strategies of financial exchanges and market facilities beginning in the early 2000s was to deliver some high-quality 'underlying' (as practitioners of financial valuation call that substrate) to very demanding clients in search of price masses to crunch. These were the large investment banks that were ready to excite competition between instituted stock exchanges, threaten to use alternative trading systems, prompt mergers or, if still unsatisfied, build their own price-production plants (so-called 'dark pools', which, roughly speaking, are price-discovery platforms run internally by investment banks themselves). Stock exchanges such as the New York Stock Exchange or the Paris Bourse, which had progressively turned into data and technology vendors in the 1990s, underwent a wave of mergers and incorporations in the 2000s whose alleged purpose was (as in the case of NYSE Euronext, Inc., the last instalment so far of the fate of the institution once known as the Paris Bourse) to provide, at a low cost, flows of prices for the escalating apparatuses of derivation in investment banking. So it seems that this is the particular kind of prices that price discovery automation ended up constructing: prices progressively extracted from the logic of commercial transaction and sold as quantitative bulk matter to feed the crafts of the financial underlying.

5 Testing consumer preferences

There are many things that market researchers and marketing professionals cannot look at directly, things that are instrumental to them and to their clients, but that cannot be easily grasped out in the wild and need to be obtained instead through the crafts of the artificial. The 'preferences' of 'consumers' are among the most significant of those things. I use quotation marks for these notions because I consider both the act of being a consumer and the fact of having a preference as performative achievements that are prompted within a marketing elicitation device. In very much the same way as an experimental protocol within the sciences provokes what it looks at in order to generate relevant knowledge, the market research setting provokes artificially, although with some acute sense of naturalism, the chemically pure occurrence of the consumer expression.

In this chapter, I refer to an ethnographic study of consumer testing in the perfume industry carried out in 2007, whose detailed results have already been published (Muniesa and Trébuchet-Breitwiller 2010; see also Trébuchet-Breitwiller and Muniesa 2010). I also use marginally some ethnographic materials gathered in 1999 on the use of methods of experimental economics in the study of consumer behaviour (see Teil and Muniesa 2006; Muniesa and Callon 2007) and a few theoretical insights elaborated elsewhere (Lezaun *et al.* 2013). What is the point here? These techniques are, of course, performative in a very straightforward sense of the word: they refer to what they provoke. The point is to see how this occurs and to understand what we are left with in terms of the realized consumer reality.

Performativity and the marketing simulacrum

Notable interest in the vocabulary of performativity has been expressed in recent contributions to the study of marketing and market research practices (e.g. Kjellberg and Helgesson 2006, 2007; Araujo 2007; Araujo *et al.* 2010; Zwick and Cayla 2011). This interest is justified by the obvious: whereas sometimes marketing practitioners are struggling to grasp an elusive and indiscernible reality, at other times this reality – of consumer behaviour, market trends and shopping desire – is explicitly conceived as the outcome of their tasks. Their job is to be performative. There is indeed a largely shared interpretation of the idea of performativity in the social studies of marketing: that marketing is performative because it has effects on markets. This is true, although not very refined. Marketing, as its name suggests, is noticeably about making markets. Still, there is a sense in which the social studies of marketing quite thoroughly meet the performative idiom that students of science once detected in the experimental sciences (e.g. Pickering 1995). Methodologies in market research provide a rich illustration of the problem of provocation, namely of the fact that the researcher learns from what she stirs, elicits, produces and activates. And, accordingly, these methodologies tend to exhibit the trouble of the provoked reality, its naturalness, its artificiality – that is, the trouble of performativity.

Focus groups constitute an illuminating example of such trouble. Javier Lezaun has inspected the combination of epistemic discomfort and epistemic efficacy that the focus group setting – a widespread methodology of market research – conveys, focusing, for instance, on 'the distinction and balance between naturalness and artificiality in the focus group setting, and the embodiment of this distinction in the moderator's skills and abilities' (Lezaun 2007a: 132). Indeed, whether they choose to emphasize the naturalness or the artificiality of the procedure, 'most moderators would nevertheless argue that, in the practical conduct of a focus group, both dimensions need to be tackled and made compatible' (Lezaun 2007a: 134). The situation is paradoxical: the strength of the focus group technique rests on the ability to extract authentic individual opinions through a heavily orchestrated group device. The well-trained facilitator is well trained insofar as she can cope with the tension between 'the natural validity of the product the focus group strives to generate and the experimental nature of its extraction' (Lezaun 2007a: 135). In short, the crafty moderator understands the performative nature of the focus group effect, and copes with it.

The very notion of 'focus group effect' was elaborated by Catherine Grandclément and Gérald Gaglio in order to push this sort of reflection further. Focus groups, they observed, are revered in marketing circles in part because they provide marketers and clients with the unique opportunity to observe 'real consumers' (so to say) and access their spontaneous inner selves 'in the flesh'. This is rendered in quite a spectacular manner indeed in the focus group setting, which includes the privacy of the observer's back room and the proverbial two-way mirror of the focus group facility. But, Grandclément and Gaglio indicated, the very incongruity of 'an encounter that is characterized by prevention of interaction by way of a physical obstacle, namely the obscured or mirrored window, sheds a telling light on the paradoxical "reality effect" of the device of the focus group' (Grandclément and Gaglio 2011: 88). That is indeed the crux of the effect achieved by the focus group: that of producing the surprising effect of exhibiting 'real consumers' as rare and unique. Focus groups, the authors wrote, are thus 'literally spectacular; their scripted nature, their theatrical display – all these elements are there to provoke the thrilling experience for a marketer of watching a consumer without being seen' (Grandclément and Gaglio 2011: 104).

It makes sense, we notice again, to consider the focus group from a performative angle. The focus group is a performance in both the sense of staged play (it possesses the traits of a scenic device) and of an exploit (the moderator will display more or less remarkable skills in eliciting consumers' opinions). But, as the authors argue, performing something is about 'making the thing happen for real; it is about provoking material realities and not merely about staging a play or accommodating collective representations' (Grandclément and Gaglio 2011: 107). But what kind of reality is this?

What if we say that the focus group is a simulacrum? That can sound critical enough: a Baudrillard-infused disavowal of the postmodern crisis of truth. But we know by now (I hope) what we miss if we take that path. Not that the focus group is not a simulacrum; it is a simulacrum, very much indeed. But it is a simulacrum insofar as the simulacrum is a vehicle of effectuation, as Deleuze would have liked to put it (Deleuze 1968a, 1969). The 'focus group effect' is not an effect in the sense of a delusive appearance, but in the sense of a productive realization. What happens inside the focus group is of course not meant to be a replica of what happens elsewhere (say, in the market). To call that a bad copy of the original is either to side with a quite Platonist understanding of the simulacrum (an understanding that simulacrum-makers can sometimes share in discourse but never in practice if they want to succeed in making a difference) or to miss entirely what is happening in terms of the production of reality.

What the focus group produces, to a great extent and on quite an industrial scale today, is the habitual experience for thousands of marketers of exerting their trade in consumer figuration. It produces a cultural medium: the very cultural medium in which objects for consumption can be safely plunged, a site for industry participants to consider, display and articulate these objects, a space in which marketing practitioners can develop their own professional worldviews and their own marketing selves. Considered as a simulacrum, which is what it is, this technique does not produce a more or less flawed representation of markets, but the very cultural matter required for the production of marketing. That is so, unless we consider that what makes markets should not be considered as constitutive of what markets are about (but that is not very advisable).

The 'market' is not a distant site, a spot located apart from that medium. The market is inside that medium. The focus group is just one example. I am referring more generally to the myriad forms of simulacra in which particular instances of the market are enacted over and again. Qualitative and quantitative market research and consumer testing techniques constitute a varied universe, to which one can add strategy, financial analysis and countless other instruments of market preparation (Callon *et al.* 2007). Can one imagine a consumer market without them? No, precisely because their purpose is to imagine markets. Now substitute 'imagine' for 'realize' and you will get even closer to a performative understanding of markets. And all this is an empirical matter: one just needs to wonder where consumer markets would be without these accumulations of simulacra (nowhere, literally).

Taming the test, taming the market

Consider the following scene. Participants arrive at the testing site, a sober, rather gloomy room located in the basement of a Parisian hotel. Their identity cards are verified by an employee of the recruitment agency, and they are shown to their tables (Muniesa and Trébuchet-Breitwiller 2010; Trébuchet-Breitwiller and Muniesa 2010). There are 40 of them, seated in four rows of 10 participants each, all facing the front of the room. Each participant finds a pen, a questionnaire and a small plastic capsule in front of her. The capsule has an abstruse code written on the lid (e.g. 'G47'), and contains an absorbent medium soaked with perfume. Twenty different fragrances are hence to rotate from seat to seat and from row to row during the testing session (and from 'consumer' to 'consumer'). The session will last more than an hour. A facilitator steps in and provides instructions on how to proceed, as well as a few explanations on the conduct and purpose of the test.

This is a blind test. The different fragrances are to be identified only through the code written on the lid. They may correspond to perfumes currently under development or to already commercialized products. Participants need to smell the perfumes and fill out the questionnaire. This is a quantitative questionnaire with a standard hedonic scale ('I like it/I don't like it') and a set of two-sided scales for perceptual and interpretive terms (pairs such as 'dark/bright' and 'hard/soft' alongside pairs such 'feminine/masculine' or 'for the day/for the evening'). Participants are given a few minutes to rate the perfumes using these scales before they move on the next capsule. At the end of the session, each participant receives a small compensation in the form of a gift voucher. Results thus gathered are then compiled and treated statistically in order to characterize each tested fragrance – its so-called hedonic performance. This input will inform the marketing strategy and manufacturing adjustments, and contribute to the shaping of the market in a decisive way.

The scene might seem odd if one expects it to correspond to an investigation on mundane perfume wearing and perfume shopping. But this is a constitutive scene of the perfume industry today. Such kinds of tests occupy the world of perfume marketing on a massive scale. Perfume brands and the companies to which they belong (holding companies usually positioned in the luxury or cosmetics sectors) commission these types of tests routinely. So do perfume manufacturers, that is, the fragrance laboratories that are specialized in the production of olfactory compositions for the perfume industry. For example, these tests enable brands to sort out fragrances from a set proposed by fragrance laboratories as candidates for a new branded perfume, and pick up the most suitable, that is, the one that records a most satisfactory hedonic performance. The brand can also use test results to commission an alteration of the proposed fragrance in order to adapt to marketing requirements.

The test is a competition, not just mere preparation for it. The testing campaign produces the space in which perfume producers and the fragrances they produce find themselves enmeshed in a competitive process, plunged within this artificial medium of hedonic performance. It is quite hard, I believe, to find an instance of a market simulacrum that better illustrates the fact that what is done within this medium is not a pale and possibly defective copy of what ought to take place out there, somewhere in distant reality, but a productive realization, an immanent establishment – in this case, of competition between fragrances against the background of mass consumer expression and, hence, of the perfume market. It is to be noted that the input generated with such techniques governs, to a great extent, the strategic decisions that translate into the mass production, global marketing and extensive wearing of tons of branded perfume based on this fragrance and not that one.

If these tests do actually enact the market, it is of course very much advisable to actually be the one commissioning the tests and setting them up. One calculates better in a calculative space that one has been able to configure (Callon and Muniesa 2005). Since the advent of perfume mass-marketing around the 1970s, consumer testing practices have been driven by perfume brands, introduced and mastered by them. One thing that is perhaps not clear for many perfume users, including some reading these pages, is that perfume brands do not manufacture their own perfumes. The mixtures of aroma compounds are created by fragrance manufacturers whose laboratories are specialized in the production of olfactory compositions. Major players in the field are firms such as Givaudan, IFF (International Flavors & Fragrances) and Firmenich. Perfumers working for or in the laboratories of these firms develop fragrances that are tested for and selected by a specific brand. For example, IFF would submit a series of fragrances and Dior, the brand, would pick up one for the development of, say, Dior Homme. IFF would then produce the aroma compound for Dior, or more exactly for LVMH, the holding company. And, of course, when submitting candidate fragrances, IFF would be inclined to submit fragrances that are likely to perform well in the tests commissioned by Dior. So why not test them prior to the Dior test, using comparable testing techniques? Fragrance firms do actually conduct testing campaigns to identify the fragrances that should be submitted to testing campaigns. Mass-market perfumes are entangled within these layers of tests, hence constituted through this *mille-feuilles* of simulacra.

Testing well, we see, is a central concern within the perfume industry. And the way the industry and its products are shaped depends heavily on it. One can even conjecture that a major focus on statistically relevant hedonic performance may translate into the production of fragrances that tend to smell alike (Trébuchet-Breitwiller and Muniesa 2010). A concomitant strategy emerges, though, which consists precisely in escaping this logic: some perfume brands choose indeed to singularize their products through the so-called 'niche' trajectory, one that explicitly puts a ban on marketing tests and uses the perfumer's own creative criteria as the primary input for the determination of the fragrance composition. But the bulk of what is done in this sector goes through the testing site. Perfumers may try to escape the weight of the tests developed by brands by developing their own testing techniques instead of just replicating them. Indeed, a particular testing technique carries a particular script, a particular repertoire of achievement, a particular emphasis on this and that criterion.

The test examined here is an example of a perfumer testing technique trying to counter, or at least balance, the methods used in brand testing techniques (Muniesa and Trébuchet-Breitwiller 2010). As put forward in the specialized literature in cognitive psychology and neurophysiology (e.g. Dubois 2000, 2006; Rouby *et al.* 2002), vocabulary is an issue in the expression of olfactory characteristics. Participants who filled out questionnaires in the scene described earlier found themselves exposed to both scents and words. The questionnaire is, in a sense, the scene of a battle, or perhaps rather of a compromise, between alternative lexicons: that of marketers and that of perfumers. In a questionnaire favouring the perfumer's technical vocabulary (and, hence, the skills and agenda of fragrance firms) the idea would be to assess the fragrance in terms of smell: 'fruity', 'woody', 'spicy', 'floral', etc. This sort of terminology is of course open to imagination, but it also corresponds to technical terms used by trained perfumers in order to describe elements constitutive of the odorant composition. The marketer's vocabulary (and, hence, the one favoured by perfume brands) is oriented toward attitude, usage and image: 'modern', 'masculine', 'sexy', 'for the evening', etc. An overemphasis on this type of wording tends to place the perfume in the territory of marketing professionals, excluding perfumers from the discussion. In the test referred to above, the idea was to rely on a sort of an intermediary vocabulary that could be used in order to trade meaning between both idioms: a 'sensory' vocabulary, as the authors of the test put it, as opposed to either a 'technical' one, i.e. perfumer-oriented, or an 'emotional' one, i.e. marketer-oriented; that is, a sort of a perceptual, experiential vocabulary combining pairs such as 'dark/bright' and 'hard/soft' (the trick is that these convey both material reality and impressionistic interpretation). Again, if there is a medium in which the balance of strength that configures the market should be enacted, it is the test questionnaire.

Becoming a measuring instrument

What happens to participants inside the testing venue? What do they do? The easy answer is, they are consumers; they express their preferences, so they act as proxies for the real market and the test records that. An ethnographic examination of what actually happens inside the testing venue tends to blur that answer a little. Participants do act as surrogates for something else, indeed; but this acting is an active performance, and active alteration of oneself. Participants we talked to thought of themselves as acting 'naturally' (as the facilitator actually requested of them), but they also repeatedly employed the vocabulary of learning and performing – and of becoming. The test did not measure something inside of them, rather the test turned them into 'measuring instruments'. Some used that expression, which we found remarkable.

Acquiring swiftness and aplomb in their judgements, reaching a sense of self-coherence and soundness but also of automatism and spontaneous instinct, experiencing the exercise as a form of olfactory training, wondering about their quality as testers: all these elements were considered by participants as important features of their performance. 'Their performance' was explicitly important for some, who were indeed interested in the whole business of becoming an olfactory measurement device. One for example told us: 'I would really like to be told about the composition of the fragrances we are testing, to compare it with what I felt myself ... I wonder if participating in these tests could help developing one's nose' (Muniesa and Trébuchet-Breitwiller 2010: 330). Another one wondered about 'his historical files', as if the testing firm had kept records of his performance as a measurement instrument. To them, 'performance' meant their performance as measurement instruments of their own personal impression, but also their performance as measurement instruments of the characteristics of the perfumes they were exposed to. Most of the observed participants found it easy to achieve this act. Many told us something along the lines of: 'The first time, I was a bit apprehensive because I thought I wouldn't manage to do it well. But it's easy actually. You just have to trust your intuition' (Muniesa and Trébuchet-Breitwiller 2010: 328).

One thing that struck us as most salient in relation to the problem of the interplay between naturalness and artificiality (a recurrent puzzle in matters of performativity, as we have seen before) was the efforts that both facilitator and participants put into neutralizing reflexivity. Becoming a measurement instrument of one's own preferences implies indeed reflecting about what they are, at least a little bit. One has to interrogate oneself. And this is an active operation, one that is likely to take time (especially if one has never asked oneself such kinds of questions). But there is no time, and this is an essential element in the dosage of reflexivity in the testing device, or rather in its paradoxical neutralization. The pace of the test made any reflexive attitude unlikely, and that was on purpose. The facilitator could even reproach a too intense involvement in the act of interrogating oneself: 'You wonder whether you'll buy the perfume or not, when all you've got to do is smell and note down'. A proper achievement of the active task of becoming an effective participant requires putting oneself in a somewhat passive position, without asking oneself questions. A participant explained, 'When we participate several times, well, it's always the same, and in a way the advantage is that we do not need to think, we smell the perfume at a reflex level'. Reflexivity is in order, but in the sense of reflex, not reflection.

The reason many participants found it easy to do that was perhaps linked to the fact that they were used to participating in such kinds of tests. Readers acquainted with the methodological rules of consumer testing might find it odd to discover that most of the observed participants did not correspond to the ideal 'candid subject' favoured in social-scientific experimental protocols. Many of the participants were actually quite used to consumer testing. Some were regulars, and even seemed to know each other. Why did the facilitator not try to screen those people out? The recruitment procedure could not bypass the fact that social networks were forming among people interested in participating in such tests: people who are interested in wearing perfume and having access to free samples, people who are interested in meagre but nonetheless useful sources of income (e.g. the gift voucher). It was quite inevitable that participants were sometimes far from fresh, 'candid subjects'. But that was not presented as a serious flaw. On the contrary, quite interestingly, this was implicitly considered by the team in charge of the test, in part, as some sort of a guarantee on the reliability of participants, that is, on the reliability of their performance as measuring instruments. If you want good measurement equipment, it should be prepared and rehearsed.

The explicit methodological reasoning used by test practitioners is inherited from a modernistic appraisal of social science and is, of course, not compatible with the idiom of performativity: you want to bring sample consumers to the laboratory, measure their olfactory preferences, and rule out any kind of bias, in particular any induced by familiarity with the experimental protocol. But this is not quite what happens. The tacit, unspoken reasoning, the one that is required by the need to have in practice a robust and effective testing device, is more consistent with the ethnographic observation: participants become measuring instruments in a situation that requires a crafty adjustment of reflection and reflex, and an active interest in the accuracy of the process.

I should perhaps note that this kind of implicit scientific epistemology is consistent with the understanding of experimental diplomacy developed by authors such as Vinciane Despret (2004a, 2004b), who firmly defended the scientific interest of using experimental participants who are interested in the research questions they need to answer, as opposed to the anti-bias ideology of deception famously put forward in experimental psychology (Korn 1997). We start perhaps to better understand the width of the breach once exposed by Bruno Latour (1991, 1993a) between the epistemology of naturalistic discovery at work within the ideals of modern science (the bias-free revelation of consumer preferences, in the case under scrutiny here) and the empirical account of the institutive reality of modern experimental methodologies (here, the performative provocation of a state of measurement). We also see that what happens in this empirically consistent reality is not a pile of undetected biases and untruthful arrangements, but the very advent of sound, relevant testing. There is no elicitation without provocation. There is no testing without performance. The professionals that developed this particular perfume test were a bit shy about the fact that they were entirely relying on their ability to cultivate participants' ability to become measuring instruments and to therefore force an act that is quite far from candid. But that is what it was about.

The experience of elicitation as provocation

Participant observation is an interesting resource for understanding how these kinds of processes come about. Of course, observing how one is performing as a participant in the test is precisely what the testing methodology is not about: observation counters the neutralization of reflexivity that the testing device ought to cultivate. But it is worthwhile to try. Acting as 'experimental subjects' in a social-scientific experiment or a consumer test and then elaborating on this unusual ethnographic material is not a common practice. To my knowledge, there is not much research on this, apart from the study described here (I was there, sitting in the testing venue, sniffing perfume and filling out questionnaires) and a previous, companion study based on the experience of participating in a study using experimental economics (Teil and Muniesa 2006). In the experimental study, experimental subjects (myself among them) were required to give a price at an auction, a form of expressing 'consumer preferences' that is particularly cherished by economists (a description of scientific context and output by the experimenters is available in Noussair *et al.* 2002, 2003, 2004a, 2004b, 2004c). The point of the experiment was to assess consumer reaction to foodstuff labelling based on 'willingness to pay' (that is the concept put forward by experimental economists). I do not shy away from my mixed feelings on the use of the researcher's personal experience as a way to prompt the reader's scientific discovery. But here we go. Can I myself hold on to the claim that having 'consumer preferences' is a performative achievement that is prompted within an elicitation device, as I claimed in the introduction to this chapter? Can I do that in the light of my own exposure to a couple of elicitation devices? The answer is yes (and my apologies for the self-centred tone in what follows).

I do like perfume. There are some perfumes that I like more than others, and there are perfumes that I particularly dislike, whether worn by others or myself. All of this sounds as if I have consumer preferences. But what I certainly know is that I did not know which perfume I prefer from a set of, say, 20 samples until I was put in a position in which I had to come up with an answer to that very question. I had to make up my mind, and I noticed how literally this idea of 'making up one's mind' is to be understood. I also knew for sure that the conditions in which I carried out the investigation heavily affected my answer. What I expressed in the consumer testing venue is, I believe, entirely different from what I would have expressed in a perfume shop or in an laboratory auction, not because I would have felt differently in those places, but because what ought to be expressed was contingent to the expression device. I also am not sure that what I said I liked is what I really like, because I know that I change, as does the way I am affected by perfume, and also because I know that I can hesitate. I could have very well revised my claims. But I also think that the exercise helped me come up with something to feel, think and say. It brought me some new bit of subjectivity, so to say (and I sincerely think it did). Yes, it provoked something in me. It forced me to have something that approaches this thing that we call a preference.

That is just about the 'I like it/I don't like it' part. Things got even more performative with the 'dark/bright', 'hard/soft' and the 'feminine/masculine', 'for the day/for the evening' parts. I had to realize (realization is definitely the word) that I could express a judgement on a perfume in terms I had never found relevant before. New problems appeared in my mind, new states of affairs that I had to settle as they came. I had to learn. After a moment in which I tried to be quite reflexive (e.g. 'I like it, but I think it's a women's perfume, and I'm a man, so should I think in terms of liking it on a woman or liking it on myself?'), I understood that the only way to cope with the pace was to rely on the intuitive automatisms that the facilitator insisted upon. I did have to stabilize my own template of calibration, my own rules for becoming a measurement instrument. At the end of the day, I had a novel, personal understanding of what 'dark/bright' or 'hard/soft' could mean for the assessment of a perfume and, perhaps, of the correlation that these criteria may have with my 'I like it/I don't like it' choices – although I am not certain of this and I did not keep track of my performance. In retrospect, I think I can say that one of my favourite perfumes (one that I particularly like to wear and, incidentally, to buy) is rather 'dark' and 'soft'. That is, I believe, one expression of my preference: a performative achievement that is prompted within the elicitation device.

Then consider that I am prompted to express myself in other terms, for example in the terms of a price that I am willing to pay in order to purchase something. It is true that I may go to the shop and purchase my favourite perfume (the one that I now know is 'dark' and 'soft' to me). I may decide not to buy it if I find it is too expensive, or I may just say 'Why not?' and treat myself. But I surely know that I have no idea of the exact price that I would use as a threshold for deciding my course of purchase. I certainly do not have inside me that thing that economists call 'reserve price'. I just may buy it or not. It depends, and I surely know that I do not know on what it depends. This looks quite contingent to me, certainly not related to some inner valuation of mine that the right configuration (e.g. a free market where I can change the price, by bidding, for example) would reveal. I know, however, from experience what happens (at least what happens to me) when one is plunged into a setting in which a 'reserve price' ought to be provoked. An experimental auction would be such a setting, one in which the price of purchase is affected by the price I declare I'm ready to pay. This is, of course, an extremely odd situation in ordinary life. But appropriate auction mechanisms are used routinely in order to elicit 'willingness to pay', a potent proxy for 'consumer preferences', that is, preferences expressed in the language of market prices.

I participated in an experiment that aimed to determine how labelling the presence or absence of genetically modified organisms (GMOs) in food would affect the expression of consumer preferences. We participants were given a humble endowment that we could use in order to bid in an auction for a cereal bar that we had tasted, bidding both before and after the disclosure of the actual packaging, which gave indications on the presence of GMOs. I could have very well made a statement on that, but I was instead required to express myself through the auction protocol, a particular protocol (a so-called Vickrey auction) that was particularly suitable for the expression of the true 'reserve price' as opposed to other protocols that exacerbate strategic gaming and non-disclosure of the true 'reserve price'. I remember perfectly that I did not have such a reserve price, but that I ended up making one up. Was it a 'fake' one? No, mine was fully compliant with the lengthy pedagogical instructions that were given to us by the facilitators. I honestly think it provided a neat expression of what I was ready to pay for that cereal bar. The device certainly provoked and produced in me something new, something that I had never experienced before: my willingness to pay, as expressed in the form of a reserve price used in order to participate in a Vickrey-type experimental auction with money that had been given to me by the experimenters. That is, I believe again, one expression of my preference: a performative achievement that is prompted within the elicitation device and that, accordingly, sharpens the particular type of subjectivity provided to me by the device. Thank you.

The sociology of market testing

A number of notable contributions to the social understanding of technological testing have emphasized the problematic distance that exists between what is produced inside the testing venue and what this is meant to refer to outside. They focused indeed on the efforts that such practices require in terms of overcoming that distance. They examined how projections linking the tested object (that is, what is done in the testing environment) and the object of the test (or, as often is said, the 'real thing') are worked out (see MacKenzie 1989; Pinch 1993; Sims 1999). This problematic relation is, of course, not dissimilar from the one that characterizes scientific experimentation (Lezaun 2007b). And it represents yet another instance of the problem of the simulacrum, as outlined in these pages. The epistemic utility that the test (or the experiment, for that matter) gains from the very fact of being set up away from ordinary hubbub requires a relationship to be traced between the facts that are articulated in the controlled setting and the uncontrolled reality that the test is meant be a test of, be it retrospective, current or prospective.

In his seminal study on nuclear missile tests, Donald MacKenzie rightly noted a crucial tension in the practical answer to the question 'Is the test situation, say, sufficiently like use to allow inferences to flow?' (MacKenzie 1989: 414). The candid answer would be to construct testing as a repetition, an exact copy of the matter under consideration; but testing requires, in fact, control conditions, safety precautions and a number of other factors, 'precisely those things that might make testing *unlike* actual use' (MacKenzie 1989: 414, emphasis in original). Something needs to be done, then, about the relationship (of likeness and unlikeness) that is constructed between the test and the actual thing.

In his programmatic contribution to the sociology of testing, Trevor Pinch insisted on the relevance of the vocabulary of projection in order to make sense of this: 'The act of projection – whether from the present to the future, from the present to the past, from the particular to the general, from the small to the large (as in miniaturization) – depends crucially upon the establishment of similarity relationships' (Pinch 1993: 29). Rather than pursuing that path through the angle of similarity judgements, rhetoric constructions and cognitive conventions, relevant research in science and technology studies has tended to consider projection as a materially mediated and embodied operation, as a 'chain of practices' in the words of Benjamin Sims, who emphasized the circulation of persons and things across different work settings (Sims 1999: 489–90).

Putting all of this in terms of translation is also a nice alternative, one that insists on the performative endeavour of the act of establishing relationships. This alternative has been investigated extensively throughout actor–network theory: reality does not travel well without material, generative operations of translation, and this applies to the claims that circulate within and outside the experimental site. The very idea of translation (*traduction* in French), in part attendant on the thought of Michel Serres in the early 1970s, was at the centre of Michel Callon's early conceptual experiments in the sociology of science (Callon 1976; Serres 1974), and was later developed into a famous case study on scallops (Callon 1986a, 1986b) and into a set of ideas that caused a little revolution in the way science is understood (Latour 1987).

The empirical starting point for this 'sociology of translation' (Callon's early formulation of what later became known as 'actor–network theory'), is best understood as a set of 'problematic statements', which are embedded in a number of settings and which characterize a series of participating entities – these are said to be problematic in the sense that they demand resolution. An operation of translation, in Callon's sense, is a process that transforms one particular problematic statement by formulating it in the terms and language of another particular problematic statement. This operation of translation, it is said, transforms the configuration of the relationships that link statements to one another. It also transforms content proper (*traduttore, traditore*). It generates new acting capacities, new referential ventures and new empirical realities. Here is what happens when testing and its projection work are considered from this vantage point: what happens inside the testing venue amounts to a series of problematic statements (e.g. 'this fragrance records the highest hedonic performance' or 'participants can express their personal preferences quantitatively') that undergo more or less felicitous operations of translation within the testing venue, but also externally in order to meet the terms of problematic statements that characterize other sites, outside the testing venue (e.g. 'this perfume is a blockbuster' or 'men do not like dark, soft perfume'). These operations produce knowledge: to know things is to operate schemes of transformation on the ensembles that contain them. But they also require the formation of a welcoming reality: operations of translation amount to the creation of metric connections, the development of habits and the circulation of objects. When something is subject to testing, it is indeed a thing to which something happens in the testing laboratory; but it also translates something else, distant from the testing laboratory. The problem of the distance between the test and the tested is not to be solved through a faithful copy of the original, but through the proliferation of operations of translation that can be severely transformative.

The sociology of markets meets here an interesting support for the understanding of the 'test drive' – an appropriate expression (Ronell 2005) – that governs its subject matter. In market testing (consumer tests, market research and other forms of experimental methodologies), the overall objective is to know 'the market', 'the consumer' or 'the product'. The problem, obviously, is that of the surrogate: the proxy through which these entities can be exposed. The simple idea according to which tested fragrances would be proxies for marketed perfumes and test participants would be proxies for actual consumers is, at best, a short cut – at worst, a blatant misunderstanding. It also leaves itself open to the standard criticisms: what is done in the test has little to do with what is actually going on in the market; it is not realistic, a simplification, a reduction of reality, a bad copy of the original. And the truth is that participants engage in a series of rather odd activities that are not exactly about acting as a consumer: clarifying the meaning of a series of impressionistic words, exercising self-coherence in the task of quantitative assessment, pacing themselves in smelling substances and filling out a questionnaire, and so on. Nobody does that in 'the market'. Does that mean that participants acted badly as proxies and that the test was flawed? Rather, it means that the test was not about representing consumers in a faithful, direct manner.

The test is, first, about turning a series of participants into instruments that measure their reactions to different fragrances. The test is a process of effectuation. What gets measured is what is effected within the strictly delineated framework of the proposed olfactory and interrogatory assemblage. This implies a series of operations of translation that happen within the testing device proper. For example, states provoked by the encounter between an odorant substance and the person sniffing it need to be transformed into the terms proposed by the questionnaire. The questionnaire, by the way, is precisely the outcome of an explicit reflection on translation, so to say, since it provides a space in which the vocabulary of perfumers and the vocabulary of marketers are dovetailed by a third type of vocabulary, as indicated above. And the questionnaire does precisely that: operations of translation. Those types of vocabularies prompt different interests, different courses of action, different realities.

Second, the test is about producing a quantitative characterization of the hedonic performance of each intervening fragrance. Again, this is the outcome of a series of operations of translation. For example, questionnaires (each characterizing one single participant) are bundled together, and then relevant data is extracted and transformed, transported to a statistical apparatus that singles out charts of hedonic performance (each characterizing one single fragrance). The chain of translations takes us from the testing venue to the locus of statistical treatment, typically taking place at the premises of a subcontracting company. A shift has occurred, one that translates into the production of composite indexes of hedonic performance that characterize a fragrance (or, as performative understanding obliges, into the production of something like the hedonic performance of a fragrance altogether). The focus is no longer on the performance of a participant as a measuring instrument, but on the performance of a fragrance as a set of attributes. Terms are different, objects are different, prompted interests and courses of action are different.

And third, the test is about clarifying what needs to be done, both on the marketing front and on the perfumery front. More operations of translation follow accordingly. For example, statements are produced that circulate outside the hedonic performance database and inform the calibration of aroma compounds and marketing campaigns. These statements carry the market, not in the sense of containing pristine bits of an otherwise unattainable empirical reality, but in the sense that they transport the virtual formulation of how the market should, can or most likely will be (since industry participants actually follow this translation). Chains of translation, which are transformative chains, are formed that link events in a testing venue with events in a database, in a laboratory and at a point of purchase. These are performative chains of effectuation, the reality which market test simulacra allow to be realized. And, by the way, you are wearing them.

6 Realizing business value

Becoming a businessperson is a quite demanding process. This process requires the assimilation of ideas and techniques that, although not breathtakingly difficult to grasp, sometimes can be a bit arid. But becoming a businessperson also requires, most notably, changing the way one thinks and the way one behaves; also the way one values things. At least this is what one can gather from a glance at the stated purposes of leading business schools and at the dominant justificatory texts of business pedagogy. You learn things, but, above all, you become someone else – a leader, hopefully – and this becoming is only marginally about knowing things. It is, above all, about reaching a felicitous mentality, about acquiring a disposition. It is about achieving an anthropological transformation. It is about being. And the vehicle for this transformation is form rather than content. You become a businessperson by doing the businessperson thing, by enacting it, by facing the practical test of realization. Being is about doing, though, as emphasized throughout the insistently experiential precepts of successful instruction in business administration.

In the following pages, I pursue a reflection on this topic following directions that I have briefly sketched out previously (Muniesa 2012). The purpose is exploratory and indicative. It is grounded on a light empirical examination of a number of historical aspects of the performance of the business valuation engine and its anthropological vehicle – the trained businessperson – at the Harvard Business School. What I tell here comes basically from reading materials produced about or by this institution. The Harvard Business School is a fantastic site for an enquiry into the performativity of business. But it is a vast site, and it is difficult to decide where to start, exactly.

I direct attention here to two different but, in my view, interconnected things. The first is the experiential, somewhat pragmatist ethos that accompanied the early development and justification of the case method of instruction at the Harvard Business School, a method which is itself a simulacrum of the business act. The second is the revelatory aspect of early reasoning in business valuation, with a focus on capitalization, its pedagogy and its anthropological preparation. For both, I examine in particular the work of Arthur Stone Dewing – a crucial character in this plot. Needless to say, the underlying understanding is that what was crafted at the Harvard Business School in the early days ended up shaping, at least to an important extent, what we recognize today as appropriate business conduct.

The hermeneutics of the business subject

In the late 1970s and early 1980s, Michel Foucault became very much interested in the practices and situations in which one's capacity of accessing some sort of truth were explicitly not about accumulating knowledge, but required instead an intense work of transformation of oneself. Veracity is seen as the outcome of exercising the self, that is, as a reform of the life of the subject and as a culmination of self-knowledge. Those are the terms, for example, of Foucault's enquiry into the practical rules for the mastery of subjectivity in ancient philosophy, especially in late stoicism (Seneca, Epictetus, Marcus Aurelius), as put forward in his 1982 lectures at the Collège de France (Foucault 2001; translated as Foucault 2005). Not a very contemporary subject matter, though Foucault mentioned in passing that, of course, one could easily recognize in our twentieth century two massively impactful forms of attainment of truth that required a radical anthropological transformation to be reached through an intensive care of the self: the psychoanalytic programme and the proletarian revolution (Foucault 2001: 30–1, 2005: 28–30). He should have added business education (see also Giraudeau 2012). And he should have looked at the case method.

If the Harvard Business School is famous for anything, it is its role in the inception, development and diffusion of the case method of instruction in business administration. Myriad things have been written and said about the forms and procedures, the justifications and rationales of this widespread technique of business pedagogy (see, for example, Forman and Rymer 1999; Swiercz and Ross 2003; Contardo and Wensley 2004). But let me just summarize what this is about for the reader who may have missed, escaped or just neglected this important contribution to the formation of the business self. First the rationale, which is, in a nutshell: since business reality is more about action than about knowledge, the right way to educate the business student is to bring business reality inside the classroom and have the student participate in it. The case, therefore, is a real (or realistic) problematic state of business affairs that requires action to be taken and that requires the student to act as if she was the business agent.

Business school students are given a copy of what is often referred to as 'the case': a document that provides some information about the 'case company', about the circumstances in which a firm and its managers are plunged, about the context in which decisions ought to be taken, all carefully written, augmented with the formulation of some questions and problems, and complemented with some figures and tables. The case, which is bought from a case publisher or prepared in-house by the instructor or by another faculty member, is the outcome of an intense work of written composition, also of detailed documentation (most of the time it is based on a real company experiencing real events, using data gathered by an assistant and shaped stylistically by the case writer). Emphasis is put on the narrative, though. Plot, protagonists, adversity, sometimes confusion, then climax (the decision point) are among the recognizable traits of an effective and relevant case. Ideally, the student has some time to prepare the case, preferably in groups, in order to come up with interpretations of situations and solutions to problems. But the real action comes afterwards, in the classroom.

The class starts with a short introduction by the instructor, who quite rapidly gives the floor to the students. The instructor is more a crafty facilitator than a teacher. Ideally, she has already prepared a strategy to orchestrate the session's dynamics: which students would be particularly fit for a 'cold call' (an opening question addressed to one student without preparation), how to naturally introduce a predefined topic, how to organize the blackboard, how to anticipate potential drifts in the discussion, and so on. She needs to take care of the session's energy – she has probably undergone specific training in order to achieve that, and put herself in quite a demanding state of awareness. The session is intensely participatory. Students themselves have to come up with arguments and decisions, be convincing and convinced. The case is not taught, but rather realized. And this realization relies on the active performance of students impersonating the business mind, for example, that of a CEO, a CFO, a top executive or top manager – a leader, in any case.

Listen to the instructor: 'What would you do if you were in that position? You, Zhang. Yes, I know, you do not have all the data you would ideally require to ground your decision. Ideally! But there is no "ideally" here. This is real life! There is no time. You have to make a decision now! And even if it is not the one best decision, you have to show us that you stick to it, that you love it. Come on, Zhang!' These are the kind of things that a visitor may hear during a case-based course at a reputable business school such as Harvard Business School: 'So, Zhang would have done that, based on that assumption. But you, Satu, you seemed to favour different assumptions. Who is right, Zhang or Satu? Dieter, yes? You have a point?' The instructor fills up the blackboard: answers, positions, percentages, also concepts and figures. At some point, the proper use of a model, a concept, an instrument or a tool can be stated by the instructor, but most likely with a pragmatic tone: 'Yes, there is this model that allows you to come up with a pretty neat guess about the right foundations for this decision, and you have to know the model. But do not forget that here you are in reality. Zhang, do you think that everybody is using that model correctly in reality? Do the competitors that you have in front of you have this model? What are they thinking? I can tell you that I don't know. Do you?' The instructor usually highlights the emergent, collective nature of the precious bits of realization that happen in the performance of the case: 'Okay, listen, if you got what Dieter just said, you got it spot on. Thank you, Dieter!' Applause follows. If things go well (because a case teaching session can turn bad, become infelicitous, not work well) students leave the classroom with a sense of excitement, with the feeling of having undergone an experience. This can surely be an entertaining experience, but sometimes also a deeply transformative one, too, especially for the ones who dare, for the ones who display the mental courage to stand up and defend their business views in an articulate and brilliant manner, i.e. the ones who find there, emerging, their business selves.

You may be wondering why I have not used the world 'simulacrum' so far, right? Indeed, here we are. A simulacrum of the business act: really doing it, though not for real, so as to be able to bear it. A performance of the live act of business. Is not what lies beneath the very idea of 'courage to act' what the would-be businessperson ought to embrace? Is it not about enduring business decision? The expression 'courage to act' is there, explicitly stated in the zealous, sometimes openly evangelical texts advocating for the Harvard case method (e.g. Garvin 2003: 60). And this courage to act is precisely what is to be exercised in the classroom. Yes, indeed, one can wonder why Foucault did not think about the case method as the prime technology for the care of the business self.

The recognizable tenets of the case method (experiential, participatory, dialogic, liberal, unrestrictive, therapeutic, realistic, practical) in business education have been apparent since the beginning. The method was developed in the 1920s, a few years after the creation of the Harvard Business School, that is, the Graduate School of Business Administration of Harvard University (Copeland 1958; Cruikshank 1987; Khurana 2007; Anteby 2013). Early proponents of the method, Wallace B. Donham in particular, resoundingly claimed inspiration from case teaching in legal education, at the Harvard Law School in particular (Donham 1922). But the blend of pragmatism that permeated the business version of what a case ought to be was quite a bit more marked than the one that could be spotted in the method famously crafted by Christopher Columbus Langdell at the Harvard Law School, which rather consisted of a logical analysis of judicial opinions that relied, in fact, on a rationalist view of doctrinal consistency and the deductibility of principles (Purcell 1973: 75). Donham's insistence on the precedent set by legal education may have been simply a strategic justification, an overstatement at any rate (Christensen 1981: 7). At the business school, hardly any rational, doctrinal principles existed that cases could be cases of. Cases would rather present themselves as instances of practical problems faced by business executives in action: the word 'problem' was actually preferred to 'case' in initial uses and early educational material (Copeland 1958: 254–62). And some kind of a pragmatist spur was definitely at work within this emerging tradition.

Arthur Stone Dewing, a highly regarded professor of economics and finance at (and one of the founders of) the Harvard Business School, was the author of a notable and often cited (and reprinted) introduction to the case method which provides one quite early occurrence of the notion of 'courage' (if not the first) in the justification of the practical, simulated exercising of the business act: 'resourcefulness, mental courage, confidence in the untried' (Dewing 1927: xxi, also 1931: 10, 1954: 5). His work gives, I think, the flavour of what I mean by 'some kind of a pragmatist spur' in the inception of early business pedagogy at Harvard. Dewing was indeed also (and before teaching finance) a professionally established philosopher, author of an *Introduction to the History of Modern Philosophy* and of an essay on *Life as Reality* (Dewing 1903, 1910). A cursory glance at those works does not provide evidence of straight obedience to pragmatism, in the sense of philosophical doctrine that was emerging at that time. On the contrary, Dewing, who was sometimes explicitly critical of pragmatism (Dewing

1910: 130–9), was rather a philosopher of an idealist kind, closer to Josiah Royce than to, say, William James – and definitely at odds with Charles Sanders Peirce. Absorbed by introspective individualism and vital intensity, Dewing's philosophy posited lived experience as the prime vehicle for the attainment of reality. That indeed has little to do with the doctrine invented by Peirce. But it is nonetheless quite compatible with the kind of intellectual atmosphere that often has been associated, at least in popular accounts (Menand 2001), with the early pragmatists and which definitely occupied quite an important space within North American neo-pragmatist circles, such as the one formed by Richard Rorty (but see Haack 1996). Forget about truth, look into purpose; forget about knowledge, look into action.

It is interesting to observe how Dewing, once converted to the pedagogy of business, found in the case method a suitable medium for this kind of philosophical impulse: education is about 'acquiring facility to act in the presence of new experience', about training 'to act' rather than 'to know', about dealing with novelty rather than 'with the departing old' (Dewing 1927: xviii). In his introduction to the use of cases, which was first published as a foreword to Cecil E. Fraser's *Problems in Finance* (Fraser 1927), he would even dare to use the cool aphorism attributed to Heraclitus, πάντα ῥεῖ (*panta rhei*) – 'everything flows' (Dewing 1927: xxi). And he also most evidently emphasized what was to be an outstanding characteristic of the case method: namely that it is not a technique for transmitting truth, but a device for transforming the way one thinks and enacts that thinking (Dewing 1927: xix–xx). And Dewing's was not a barren statement. The papers of Cecil E. Fraser at the Baker Library Historical Collections of the Harvard Business School, particularly the teaching records, contain profuse, annotated materials on the development of early cases (particularly in finance) and include a great deal of detailed descriptions of faculty members' teaching styles, in particular that of Dewing (Fraser's admired colleague), which was completely in line with the adventurous, existential views that Dewing was advertising in textbooks and printed materials (see also Fraser 1928).

The idea that business education was, first and foremost, about creating an existential disposition was present, with nuances, in the many texts that accompanied the development and refinement of the case method at the Harvard Business School (see in particular Fraser 1931; Andrews 1953; McNair 1954; Towl 1969). The work of C. Roland Christensen in the 1960s and 1970s was determinant in this process. It was at that point in which overemphasis was put on the education of educators at Harvard Business School. Fortifying the method meant providing case instructors with the habits and resources (and also the morals) that would guarantee a felicitous recipe in the conduct of the case experience.

In his detailed ethnography of the socialization of both faculty and students at the Harvard Business School, Michel Anteby provided valuable insights on this process (Anteby 2013). One thing freshly recruited faculty members receive immediately in order to start filling up the empty shelf space in their new offices, Anteby tells right away, is two house books edited by Christensen and colleagues (Christensen *et al.* 1991; Barnes *et al.* 1994; see Anteby 2013: 1). One of them is a revised version of a casebook on teaching with the case method that was first published in 1981 as *Teaching by the Case Method* (later, revised versions became *Teaching and the Case Method*) and which was also presented as some sort of an interim report on an 'experiment' (in Christensen's words): a series of seminars on the case method held regularly for more than 10 years, starting in the late 1960s, with the purpose of examining and refining the philosophy of the method but also, most centrally, its practical articulation (Christensen 1981). This was definitely a successful experiment in reflexivity, since the output indeed took the form of a set of cases (on how to teach with cases). From an intellectual angle, it stood also as an open confirmation of the pragmatist spur: John Dewey, whom Christensen called 'the largely unappreciated patron saint of much of the Business School's educational philosophy' (Christensen 1981: 13), was abundantly quoted in the introductory parts, and a section of his *Democracy and Education* ('Thinking in Education') was actually added as reading material to later editions (Barnes *et al.* 1994: 9–14; taken from Dewey 1916: 179–92). Indeed, one could very well imagine the early inceptors of the case method justifying its experiential ground in the terms of 'the necessity of an actual empirical situation', that is, of experience, quite beautifully defined as 'trying to do something and having the thing perceptibly do something to one in return' (Dewey 1916: 180).

Today, in the early 2010s, the legacy of this kind of pedagogical impetus is still at work at the Harvard Business School. To what extent does the purpose of business education consist in the transformation of the self? It does so to a very large extent. And to what extent does this transformation of the self require practical exercising? It does so also to an even larger extent. This answer is evident today based on recent in-house publications or conversations with faculty members. The motto 'knowing, doing, and being' recurs throughout recent contributions to the Harvard Business School's reflexive understanding of the formation of the successful business self (Datar *et al.* 2010: 103–6; Snook *et al.* 2012: xv–xvii). It comes from the military, apparently (Khurana and Snook 2004). Regardless, the important thing is that it serves quite well the performative constitution of the business subject through the craft of the case method and comparable techniques of simulacrum. The motto aptly conveys an idea of balance, with an emphasis, of course, on the 'doing' and, perhaps more importantly, on the 'being'.

The object of valuation and the intuition of capitalization

But what is it that the business self ought to realize? What is the object of the business simulacrum? What is the truth that one needs to obtain through such pedagogical crafts? There is, of course, no singular answer to that. Many things are taught in business schools, from the arrangement of human resources to the steering of marketing imagination, from the perception of wealth to the mastery of stratagem. The diverse logics of professionalization, institutionalization and legitimation of commercial and entrepreneurial activities, and of business schools too, make it difficult (and perhaps unnecessary) to spot any ultimate characterization of the business endeavour and of the 'act' in the 'courage to act'. Let us agree, however, on the fact that the valuation of business enterprises ought to constitute a most relevant habit of the talented businessperson, if not the nitty-gritty of the troubles of business conduct. Let us also agree on the fact that the purpose of this envisaged transformation (to become a businessperson) is not unrelated to the exposed aim of massive quantities of young candidates to business education all around the planet: namely, to make money.

Arthur Stone Dewing stands again as the author around whom the investigation can revolve. Dewing was certainly known to have contributed to the pedagogy of business valuation through an authoritative textbook on finance, *The Financial Policy of Corporations*, first published in five volumes in 1920 (following an earlier, provisional printing of the first two volumes in 1919), then reprinted several times, revised and thoroughly updated in multiple editions, abundantly reviewed, widely taught and read at the Harvard Business School and elsewhere, at least until its last edition, dated 1953, began to disappear from reading lists (Dewing 1920; see Muniesa 2012). Donald MacKenzie saw in Dewing's textbook the epitome of a rather qualitative approach to finance, one that focused on institutional arrangements and psychological aspects in the conduct of business that was ultimately swept away, from the late 1950s onward, by the quantitative revolution that transformed finance into the mathematized science of rational investors and efficient markets (MacKenzie 2006: 37–8, 70–4). Dewing's pedagogical undertaking was certainly of a qualitative kind: case-based, deeply attentive to human circumstances and sometimes openly critical of scientific formalism. But it played a lasting role, in my view, in imprinting into the business mind a neat and persistent intuition of what valuation ought to be about. And this neat and persistent intuition was not swept away. It rather stood as the intellectual substrate that allowed the quantitative revolution (e.g. Modigliani and Miller 1958) to just make sense. I am referring to the neat and persistent intuition of valuation as capitalization.

But what is this? Well, this is difficult to say precisely, because before it has been realized in the form of a neat and persistent intuition, this idea of valuation as capitalization is seemingly counter-intuitive – which is why a pedagogical effort is needed. Let us see what Dewing said about the valuation of 'a going business', as he often liked to say. I use here the 1926 edition of *The Financial Policy of Corporations*, since it is more explicit than the 1920 edition about this topic, and further editions become more and more explicit about the problem of valuation and the notion of capitalization (Dewing 1926: 258–77). Is the value of the business only the value of what the businessperson has ready to sell right away, for example, a warehouse and some stored merchandise, plus some cash in a bank account? No, at least not entirely nor substantially. The value of the 'going business' is rather obtained by examining its 'earning power', that is, its capacity to meet the purpose for which business is intended: to earn a profit. 'Earning power': that is Dewing's telling expression. The businessperson, Dewing told students, is 'buying earning capacity' (Dewing 1926: 264). This earning power is, of course, conjectural. It can translate into actual earnings or not. Its valuation is a prognostication. But it needs to be valued now, in the present, since it is the basis on which the businessperson ought to ground present decisions about what to do and where to go. It depends, Dewing explains, on the capacities of action that one can expect to spring from the combination of managerial ability and productive assets. The value of this combination – that is, the expression of its earning power – can benefit conveniently from an empirical look at the past earnings it generated, when available, as a proxy for the earnings that are to be reasonably expected in the future. In short, the value of the business is the present value of future earnings. From this follows that one reasonable way one can use to approximate the value of a 'going business' is through the 'capitalization of net earnings', Dewing indicated. But what does this mean?

The 'who' in 'to earn a profit' are the proprietors of the business, that is, the ones who contributed funds to the undertaking, which corresponds, as Dewing indicates, to the 'capital stock', which is, with 'debt', the crux of corporate finance (Dewing 1926: 3–7). Capital (capital stock plus debt) is the wealth employed in an undertaking to turn it into a going concern. Capitalization, 'a representation of this wealth in terms of purely artificial and, in the end, fictitious values', is the valuation of the capital (Dewing 1926: 6–7). Dewing referred the reader to William Z. Ripley, to which *The Financial Policy of Corporations* is dedicated, and quoted from his book *Railroads: Finance and Organization*: 'Capital is reality. Capitalization is merely a record of past operations and a bench mark or standard of measure for the future' (Ripley 1915: 55).

Although, perhaps it is the other way around. Perhaps reality is capitalization, after all, since it is the act of capitalization that ultimately produces the engagement of capital. Capital would be the nexus of social relationships produced by the capacity of capitalization – a vision not unrelated to the appraisal put forward by contemporary critics Jonathan Nitzan and Shimshon Bichler in their daunting, though very helpful, characterization of capitalization as an anthropological transformation (Nitzan and Bichler 2009). This reality, as Dewing himself told his readers, is of course propelled by the juristic form of the modern corporation, which establishes a scheme of rules of appropriation and capacitation (see Robé 1999, 2011). The 'operations of the law', as jurists of a pragmatist kind would have it (Purcell 1973: 76; but see also Thomas 2011), are indeed the performative key to the constitution of a social order. Here, the order of capitalization.

So, what the businessperson ought to do in order to make sense of the value of a going concern is to observe the present value of anticipated income, which is the same as capitalizing the business's earnings. This means that projections of earnings determine the value that the business has at present – the value for the businessperson, it is implied, in the condition of the purchaser, i.e. the potential capital proprietor. These earnings projections, since they are uncertain to a greater or lesser degree, are discounted; they obey a rate of capitalization, a ratio between the envisaged earnings and the cost (that is, the value of the business, which is what later became known in the literature as 'cost of capital'). The businessperson looks at the business, at past earnings but also at its specific features, sees a return of 1000 dollars in a year's time and estimates that the business has a current value of 952.38 dollars. The flow of 1000 dollars in the future is discounted at a 5 per cent rate. This is intuitive, right?

I do not want to obviate the well-known fact that business valuation is a vast continent of methodological sophistication, of formulaic nuances, sometimes of harsh controversies. Different ways of discounting, of benchmarking, of modelling, of forecasting and of conceptualizing interweave in a colossal global industry of valuation (Nitzan and Bichler 2009: 145–214). Today, business schools are certainly at the forefront of the diffusion of valuation methodologies, starting with the standard among the standards: discounted cash flow. The reasoning embedded in all of them corresponds to a neat and persistent intuition for millions of people who have business-related jobs: bankers, financial analysts, accountants, and so on (e.g. Ortiz 2011, 2012, 2013a, 2013b, 2013c). But this took some effort. Dewing did not invent all of this, of course. But a look at the different editions of *The Financial Policy of Corporations* provides some evidence of the intellectual energy that it took for someone like Dewing, for example, to provide apt demonstration and articulation of what the value of business means. A look at the teaching records at the Baker Library Historical Collections of the Harvard Business School reveals this as well. My point here is that comprehension of the nature of business value required indeed some kind of a mental shift that is best achieved by impersonating a capitalist. In order to get it, you need to change the way you think, and you do that by putting yourself in the position of someone who evaluates things as vehicles for 'earning power'.

Perhaps one quite determinant piece of evidence of the initially counter-intuitive intuition of capitalization is to be found in the writings of Irving Fisher, the economist most associated with the theorization of capital investment and the discount rate, and with the articulation of the moral, universal logics of discounting (Nitzan and Bichler 2009: 156). Looking at *The Rate of Interest* (Fisher 1907), for example, is, at least in part, an exercise in intuition. Fisher struggled to debunk current capitalistic intuitions (one being that the discount rate would correspond to some sort of a market price for investment money, another one that capital produces future income) and replace them with an ontology of the 'implicit interest rate' that everything (every capital good, every object prone to capitalization) would have. Capital does not produce income, at least not from the angle of value: value is the value of capital, and the value of capital is implied by the value of prospective income. 'The orchard produces the apples; but the value of the apples produces the value of the orchard' (Fisher 1907: 14). Capital is a claim on earnings, and its value is a measure of the power to hold to that claim – earning power, as pedagogue Dewing would simply end up stating. My hypothesis is that getting just that, in one way or another, is what the business self is about. And that contemporary financial business culture consists, substantially, in the massive accumulation of simulacra that attempt to realize it.

7 Indicating economic action

Performance targets and indicators: these are the demons of today's impulses towards a transparent, cost-efficient, governable, rational handling of economic things. We find them in all kinds of organizations. In the private sector, they usually serve management accounting and strategy precepts. In the public sector, they often accompany the orientation referred to as 'new public management'. They are almost always involved in some movement of 'reform', 'change', 'rationalization' or 'modernization', that is, they are meant to prompt or help prompt the modification (the improvement, their advocates would say) of the things they refer to. They are certainly linked, as critical commentators like to emphasize, to the political expectations of neoliberalism (at least sometimes), but you can see them informed also by quite different ideological ventures. Their performative capacity is now perhaps a commonplace among practitioners and researchers alike: performance indicators are meant to describe things, but through the describing, the things are transformed (sometimes unintentionally, sometimes intentionally). They offer a quite fertile ground for disputes and quandaries on their semiotic purpose and efficacy.

There was in the 2000s in France an important reform of public administration that situated performance indicators at the forefront of the modernization of the state. 'State' indeed is a notion that still exists in French (*l'État*) and that in Anglo-American vocabulary seems to have been collapsed into the notion of 'government' or been diluted into the idea of 'country'. The state, a diffuse and sometimes mysterious referential montage, is an instituted compound, an authority (it is an actor, definitely) that imposes rules and norms for collective existence, a locus of sovereign power and an organization for the conduct of the polity. Making the state accountable to performance metrics means identifying what the state does, how, and how well, but also how much and, most significantly, for how much. The LOLF reform (the acronym refers to an important act passed in August 2001, the 'Loi organique relative aux lois de finances') served as the basis for a radical transformation of the rules and procedures governing the French budgetary process and, accordingly, of the visibility and readability of the actions this budget is meant to serve. The LOLF turned into a massive trial of explicitness on the agency of the state, a massive experiment on the description (actually, on the self-description) of the state. In what follows, I use insight from an investigation carried out between 2006 and 2008 on the implementation of the LOLF in order to see what can be learned from this on the topic of the provoked economy (Muniesa and Linhardt 2011; see also Linhardt and Muniesa 2011a). Empirical materials come mostly from fastidious archival research at the premises of the French Ministry of Higher Education and Research. Drafts for performance indicators were collected and interpreted, as were minutes from strategic meetings, white papers, emails, budgetary frames – a paper trail through which this trial of explicitness could be explored in the area of national science. Of course, one important thread in that trail is about the economy: the economic cost, the economic impact, the economic rationale, the economic reality of the scientific action of the state.

Masses of performance targets and indicators

Masses of performance targets and indicators constitute a semiotic haze which envelops the state as a colossal attempt at accounting for the performance of its action, that is, of its agency. Talking about a 'semiotic haze' is a way to signal the often quite nebulous character of the vast task that a large number of civil servants, consultants, politicians and specialists of many kinds undertook between 2001 and 2007, the long period during which an operational translation of the principles and precepts of the LOLF had to be worked out. Literally thousands of indicators were drafted, discussed, forwarded, tested, criticized, all with various justifications and contradictions, consistencies and inconsistencies, penchants and rationales. But I use also the expression 'semiotic haze' to allude to the fact that the secular state is indeed constituted as both an ultimate reference and a refractory one, heavy yet elusive at the same time, mysterious, perhaps also monstrous – at least this is what one can gather from a look at a few savant commentaries in the historical anthropology of juristic institutions and of state paperwork (e.g. Legendre 1988, 1992; Du Gay 2000;

Joyce 2013). Both ideas (the referential agitation found in archival materials and the singularly hollow foundation of the represented state) do match together quite well. It is as if the immense call for managerial explicitness that the LOLF provoked resulted in the patent demonstration of the state's penchant for the elliptical.

The LOLF reform was chiefly considered to be a reform of public finance, a scheme for 'financial modernization' aimed at 'a revolution of the financial constitution of the state' (a popular local motto) that targeted operations related to the state's budgetary process and the rationalization of budgetary choices (see Barilari and Bouvier 2007; Bezes 2009; Corbett 2010). This involved, for example, the introduction of principles of management accounting: complete costs structures, fine-grained budgetary justification, and so on. But it was also presented as a reform of public administration. Along with the introduction of new accounting methods, it included new forms of assessment and reporting, new managerial vocabularies aimed at enhancing the accountability of the action of the state, at spreading a 'culture of performance' (another local shibboleth) so as to flesh out the ambition of moving from 'a logic of means' toward 'a logic of results' (another one). The description of public money moved alongside the description of public action, and these operations of description were managerial operations proper: that is, operations of government.

We confront here of course, in a quite straightforward manner, many concerns that have been expressed about the organizational, sociological or institutional aspects, reasons and consequences of performance measurement in the public sector (e.g. Hood 2000, 2006, 2007; Modell 2001, 2009; Townley *et al.* 2003; Du Gay 2004; Chapman 2005; Bevan and Hood 2006; Lascoumes and Le Galès 2007; Arnaboldi and Azzone 2010; Pipan and Czarniawska 2010). We also recognize in performance assessment the kinds of things that Jean-François Lyotard indicated about the performativity of postmodern knowledge (performance assessment serving as a paramount illustration of what he understood by that); namely, that besides serving as an instrument for government, this kind of knowledge also 'refines our sensitivity to differences and reinforces our ability to tolerate the incommensurable' (Lyotard 1984: xxv).

With the administrative parlance instituted by the LOLF, the purposes, expenditures and achievements of the state are now described in terms of 'missions', 'programmes' and 'actions'. The LOLF reform was indeed accompanied by the production and diffusion of countless glossaries and templates that attempted to clarify the new referential venture. 'Missions' are formulated in purposeful terms and correspond to broad state policies ('grandes politiques de l'État'). They relate, more or less, to the established domains of executive power, usually falling within the scope of one ministry or executive department: science, defence, agriculture, healthcare, police, education, and so on. 'Programmes' correspond to operational policy packages within each mission, each linked to specific budgetary assignments and also, usually, to a coherent segment of the public sector (departmental sections, public agencies and authorities, state institutions) and a neat distribution of responsibilities. The programme is, so to say, the unit of accountability that is submitted to parliamentarian control in the context of the approval of the yearly state budget. 'Actions' stand, inside each programme, as descriptions of concrete budgetary items associated with the intention or finality they serve, usually expressed in terms of public service or administrative conduct. An action is something that the state does, but something that demands justification and assessment in regards to its costs. Then you have 'objectives' and 'indicators'. Objectives are for a programme as a whole rather than for its actions, although some actions can be more directly recognizable in some objectives. They are formulated in terms of desired goals, and associated with indicators that can account, in a quantitative fashion, for the level of attainment of these goals.

Allow me to provide an example. 'Research and Higher Education' ('Recherche et Enseignement Supérieur') is the title of one mission. Although the Ministry of Higher Education and Research has a leading role, this is typically a mission in which other ministries also intervene. In France, there exist a number of scientific research and higher education institutions that are controlled by different ministries. The École des Mines de Paris, for example, falls within the scope of the Ministry of the Economy, Finance and Industry, and the École Polytechnique is tied to the Ministry of Defence. The official outline for the justification of the budget ('projet annuel de performances') for 2006 for the mission 'Research and Higher Education' included 13 programmes, 74 actions, 69 objectives and 139 indicators. One programme was, for example, 'Higher Education and University Research' (which basically pertained to regular state universities); others were 'Student Life' (scholarships and other aids), 'Industrial Research' (this is where they put the École des Mines de Paris, for example), and 'Space Research' (which involves the principal budget of the national laboratory for space research, the Centre National d'Études Spatiales). The programme for 'Space Research' translates into a series of actions such as 'Developing space technologies for scientific research' or 'Mastering access to space'. One formulated objective for this programme is: 'To intensify the international influence of French space research and technology'. Performance indicators associated with this objective would be, without much surprise, publication records and citation indexes, also figures for commercial exports. Another objective is: 'To guarantee a free, competitive and reliable access to space'. The associated indicators focus, it seems, on the market share and commercial profit associated with yearly launches of the Ariane carrier rocket.

In 2006, all of these missions, programmes, actions, objectives and indicators still looked a bit sketchy, fuzzy and messy. A number of commentators pointed to their problematic features, sometimes to their openly surreal characteristics (e.g. Brunetière 2006). In 2006, the first LOLF-compliant budget was presented. That was also the time when our research fieldwork began; access was granted to the archives of the office in charge of coordinating the construction of the mission 'Research and Higher Education' (Muniesa and Linhardt 2011). Of particular interest were the traces of doubts and discussions, sometimes of vivid disagreement, in the implementation process. What is the appropriate formulation for this or that programme? Is there a budgetary overlap here? What does this expenditure correspond to? Is this institution part of the state or not? Who is responsible for the conduct of this action? Is this an action of the state proper, or rather a consequence of an action of the state? Is the formulation of this objective sound and legitimate? Does this indicator really account for the attainment of this objective? Is there a bias or a misunderstanding? Are the sources needed in order to calculate this indicator known and available? Is there a conflict with an alternative source? Are there some negative consequences of the use of that indicator? Do we want this indicator of policy efforts to increase, to signal strength of commitment? Or do we want it to decrease, to signal the effectiveness of policy measures that no longer need to be overemphasized? Does this indicator need to be an economic indicator? But what does it mean for an indicator to be economic? Is something important left out? Does this or that measure serve the orientations and principles of the LOLF? What are those orientations exactly, in concrete terms? Sketchy, fuzzy, messy and hazy – these documents placed us in the midst of the semiotic haze. Things became clearer through the years, and the referential apparatus became more explicit – but only up to a certain point. The implementation of the LOLF remained a struggle for the interpretation of what the reform was (or ought to be) about.

Throughout the conception and implementation process, performance targets and indicators exhibited several of the problems of performativity that I am working out here. They met the problem of description quite straightforwardly. Describing the performance of the state amounted to formulating what the performance ought to be, and to conducting a metrological enquiry that set in motion a very proactive process. They also met the problem of explicitness. Performance targets and indicators put their object to the test of sound formulation and sparked controversies on what the object was supposed to be. They met the problem of the simulacrum, too. The semiotic haze they formed was often interpreted, especially in critical accounts, as a barren plot, but it was also undeniably taken as the medium through which the agency of state ought to be realized, rightly or wrongly. They finally met the problem of provocation, indeed provoking the advent of a novel managerial identity of the state.

At the centre of these problems (if not at the centre, then in a quite dominant position) was the problem of what I call economic indication. Something important in the LOLF movement had to do with the economic reality of the action of the state: its economic costs and rationales, its economic impacts and effects. Many of the struggles and quandaries that animated the semiotic haze were about the interpretation and implementation of an economic template for the state to express itself. The reform altogether was, in one way or another, about economizing. But what does this mean? Some interpreters put an emphasis on economic rationing and budgetary control while others cared more about economic drive and the provision of incentives. As open and potentially hollow as the notion may be (e.g. Muniesa *et al.* 2007; Çalışkan and Callon 2009, 2010; Muniesa 2010), economization and its elucidation was central to this business. A few examples follow.

Political or economic action

To what extent does an economic view of the state contradict a political one? One possible answer is, to a very large extent. At least, this is an answer one can infer from a number of critiques of managerialism and neoliberalism that identify a form of depoliticization of the action of the state in operations such as the one envisaged in the LOLF. Albert Ogien is, in France, among the most relevant critics in that line of argument, with an explicit reference to the LOLF (Ogien 1995, 2007, 2010). If this is depoliticization, and if this is presented in a rather demoralizing manner, it is because the nature of what the state is and does is essentially political, one is drawn to conclude. This resonates with a number of intellectual threads that have championed and still champion the political nature of the state. One, most famously intimidating, is of course that of Carl Schmitt, who claimed that the ideals of economic thrift and enterprise, moral individualism and the science of economics, together were the vehicles of the depoliticization of the state and, subsequently, of its potential neutralization – worse, its extermination (Schmitt 2007: 78). In a climate characterized by concerns about softness, tittle-tattle and accounting, combined with a love for states of exception and trenchant *Entscheidung*, depoliticizing the state sounded indeed like some sort of a phantasmal emasculation (see Sombart 1999). And that version of what the political nature of the state ought to be contributed effectively to the great European hallucination that resulted in the destruction of civilization, state included, in the late 1930s and early 1940s.

A more sane interpretation of what is political in the political essence of the state may side with more democratic ideals, perhaps also equally European in a way, that still see nonetheless in economic rationales the terms of the impairment of democratic political life, as exemplified recently by Jürgen Habermas and his defence of European constitutionalism in the face of the banking menace of the late 2000s and early 2010s (Habermas 2012). It is to be noted, on the controversial topic of the combinations and contradictions of a political and an economic view of the state, that the reconstruction of the German state after World War II relied precisely on watering down the political concept of the state by means of an economic conception of its institution. Michel Foucault quite cleverly referred to this process in his study of neoliberalism in the reconstruction of the German state through a social market economy as 'politics of economization' (Foucault 2004b: 248, 2008: 242; Linhardt and Muniesa 2011b). Commentators have abundantly spotted in Foucault's arguments an insistent critique of neoliberalism, but the truth is that he was referring to it, in part, as an ingredient for peace. Poor Europe, anyway.

Am I going too far with such historical references? Are the minute operations of description and indication of the action of the state in the context of a French administrative reform in the 2000s connected in some way or another with the fate of Europe? Perhaps. In any case, a number of the trials of explicitness that governed the implementation of the LOLF did resonate, at least partially, with these types of questions. The LOLF reform was definitely interpreted by some as an attempt to penetrate the core of the state with an enterprise-inspired, economy-driven managerial vision, a vision that may eventually run counter to the state's political singularity. But emphasis should be placed on the word 'attempt', on the characteristics of this attempt and on the type of context it met, or served. Philippe Bezes provided an extremely precise contextualization and theorization of the intricacies of this process (see Bezes 2005, 2008, 2009, 2012). What our research modestly attempted to elucidate was the nature and consequences of the patent ambivalence that characterized the formulation of the LOLF: in short, a formulation that could be understood by some as a plea for an economization of the state and by others as a defence of its politicization.

What the LOLF exactly was or was not was a topic of dispute in administrative and political circles. Many aspects of the reform were sometimes said to be not directly derived from the LOLF itself, but to correspond instead to 'the spirit of the LOLF'. The LOLF was characterized from its inception by some degree of ambiguity, perhaps purposefully (Linhardt and Muniesa 2011a). The passing of the LOLF Act in 2001 was characterized, surprisingly, by large parliamentarian consensus. Both socialist and conservative mainstream political forces joined together in the approval and celebration of this reform's rationale. The LOLF could be interpreted in a variety of ways. The reform could be defended very well by emphasizing economies in public spending, control of public debt, and hence the reduction of the size of the state, very much in line with an economic, neoliberal drive. But it could also be supported as a way of enhancing visibility in the voting of the public budget, and thus as a democratic grip on the budgetary discussion: the purpose was for parliamentarians to at last be in control of what the state does. Alternatively, the reform could be interpreted as a lever for the governmental orientation of public administrations, that is, as an instrument for the enhancement of the will of the state. In a nutshell, the LOLF had some of the characteristics of what Dominique Linhardt has pertinently termed an *épreuve d'État*, that is, a 'trial of state' (Linhardt 2012). These are not just situations in which the strength and characteristics of the state are put to the test. These are situations in which the very reality of the state is summoned to expression (see also Linhardt and Moreau de Bellaing 2005).

Let us see what happened, for example, with the purpose, rationale and existence of one particular programme within the mission for Research and Higher Education: the programme for the 'Orientation and Command of Research' ('Orientation et pilotage de la recherche').

In early drafts of the mission's template (sometime around 2004), a number of issues were raised about one action titled 'Training for and through research' ('Formation à et par la recherche'). From a budgetary perspective, this action was supposed to cover the grants for doctoral research controlled by the Ministry of Higher Education and Research. Two different ministerial departments, one in charge of higher education and the other in charge of research, expressed competing views about this action. The Department of Higher Education wanted to have this action made part of a programme called 'Higher Education and University Research' ('Formations supérieures et recherche universitaire'), but the Department of Research, which was in fact responsible for the management of these PhD grants, wanted to keep this action as part of the programme for the Orientation and Command of Research ('Orientation et pilotage de la recherche'). Well, yes, this was a classic case of administrative quarrels and struggles over attributions of responsibility, control and budget. But it was also an intriguing case that exposed significant drifts in the vocabulary of the political and economic characterization of the action of the state, here focused on the conduct ('orientation and command') of scientific research.

In an administrative note issued by the Department of Research, the position of the Department of Higher Education was said to favour, wrongly, 'the managerial logic of higher education institutions' and to fail to allow for 'strong political stress in terms of scientific orientation at the state level', adding that it was this 'dimension of political highlighting of a national policy for the development of the scientific capabilities needed by the nation' that justified the maintaining of doctoral grants within the aptly named programme for the Orientation and Command of Research (Muniesa and Linhardt 2011: 556–7).

Certainly, doctoral grants provide doctoral students with economic support, but it is also a way of signalling which directions new scientific ventures should take. The notion of 'strong political stress' (*affichage politique fort* in French) that we found in that document is very interesting in this regard. The literal meaning of the word *affichage* is displaying or billposting (an *affiche* is a poster), but it is also often used in French in a figurative sense. Within the context of the vocabulary of transparency in new public management, this expression can be linked to other words present in LOLF-related parlance such as 'visibility' (*visibilité*) or 'readability' (*lisibilité*). But, as a mode of 'rendering visible', the notion of *affichage* has interesting connotations: it is about signalling and capturing attention (not everything ought to be displayed, only what is of strong relevance) but also about affirming, almost about proclaiming in a trenchant manner. In addition, here the *affichage* is meant to be a strongly 'political' one.

What does 'political' exactly mean here? The 'orientation' of science does not refer to the politicization of science in the sense of fostering a partisan view of scientific reality. It refers rather to the execution of policy, that is, to an act of government. Science is 'oriented' insofar as it stands as the purposeful object of public policy, and it allows for 'strong political stress' insofar as the determined direction it follows is politically conducted. The authors of the quoted document insist on the idea that a doctorate is a research activity, and minimize the administrative requirements of a 'managerial logic' (*logique de gestion* in French). Here, 'managerial' (an openly ambivalent notion) clearly refers to an idea of administrative functioning and economic handling of the reality under discussion; it is clearly about the payroll. In another context, that very same word, 'to manage', could have been used to refer precisely to the act of orienting and commanding – the very act that the authors of the note associated with the political determination of the capacities of the state.

That almost strictly opposite meaning of 'management' is to be found in other items of our paper trail, for example in a note circulated sometime in 2003 by the Department of Budgetary Reform, a service located within the Ministry of Budget in charge of supervising the implementation of the LOLF from a budgetary perspective. The authors underlined the fact that the mission for Research and Higher Education 'does not represent a management reality' and 'is not a response to the coordination and the conduct of policies' (Muniesa and Linhardt 2011: 556–7). Emphasis was put on budgetary authorization, not on the implementation of policy. This note was most likely read as a threat to the political interpretation defended by the authors of the first one (the excerpts were heavily marked in the version that we read at the archives of the Ministry of Higher Education and Research). And still, 'management' was used here almost as a synonym of 'command' and 'orientation'. What we see here are groups of civil servants and state practitioners struggling to make explicit the politicizing or, alternatively, the economizing interpretation of the 'the spirit of the LOLF'. Expressions such as 'managerial logic' served as hollow concepts that this trial of explicitness sought to fill.

Promoters of a politicizing view of the LOLF at the Ministry of Higher Education and Research struggled to feed, in different ways, the

118 *Elementary case studies*

policy rationale of the various instruments and structures developed throughout the implementation process (see also Cytermann 2006; Eyraud *et al.* 2011). The programme for the Orientation and Command of Research was one vehicle among others used to emphasize the political meaning of public management. It seems that they somehow ended up losing that battle to some extent. The programme was 'killed', as emphatically put by an informant, for a number of circumstantial reasons. Did they also lose the war? Perhaps. It is difficult to see any big picture in the midst of the semiotic haze, but the contours seem to correspond to a shift toward an economization of the agency of the state, an emphasis on its managerial identity, a stress on the state as an 'agency' in the administrative sense of the word: an executive organization that handles economic means (incentives and disincentives) for some particular action; here, scientific research.

Quantifying scientific production

This leads us to one of our ('our' for 'us' researchers, with apologies to non-concerned readers) favourite topics of discussion: research assessment, of the quantitative kind. The statistical analysis of scientific activity and of its potential consequences has a long history of implications for science and technology policy (Godin, 2003, 2004, 2005, 2007). Scientometrics – that is, the quantitative measurement and analysis of scientific production – in recent decades has become a crucial instrument for the institutional assessment of research and researchers (Pontille and Torny 2013). Scientific production leaves traces in the form of publications (for some extremist viewpoints, scientific production amounts, in fact, to the production of these traces in and by themselves). And these traces can be analysed in terms of quantities and relationships (of and between words, texts, authors, and so on). Citation indexes are among the most widely used (and sometimes controversial) proxies for scientific importance. And they were at work within the LOLF's semiotic haze, of course. I have already mentioned one example, in the case of space research: the objective of being scientifically important is translated into scientometric indicators (quantity of publications and quantity of citations for French space research, compared to the rest of the world, roughly put).

Clever or not, this particular blend of statistical impetus can definitely relate to some particular conception of the purpose of something like the quantitative description of the action of the state. Here, guidance can be sought from Alain Desrosières, who attentively observed the correspondences between, on the one hand, several historical configurations of the state and, on the other hand, several penchants for particular statistical methods and specialities (Desrosières 2003a, 2003b). What would be the neoliberal state's favourite template for quantitative self-observation? Among its favourite terms, Desrosières suggested, would be microeconomic incentives and performance indicators (see also Bruno and Didier 2013). What would be an alternative statistical view? The most immediate contrast would be with some sort of a Keynesian state, whose favourite statistical apparatuses would be macroeconomic modelling and forecasting, perhaps also combined with the attention to national account systems that one can find in a technocratic state with a command or mixed economy (this is what many would identify as a fair definition of France, at least until the 1980s). Desrosières was less interested in any neatness of historical periodization than in the nuts and bolts of the practice of statistical production, and this angle truly matches the kind of situations that the push for scientometrics represented in the context of the LOLF. There was indeed an interesting push for scientometrics in the paper trail I am reporting on here. And, in a sense, it can very well fit into the neoliberal batch: an idea of competition between scientific fields and scientific actors, with 'market shares' to win (metaphorically, most of the time at least), and with public policies focused on the strategic monitoring of publication trends.

As a trial of explicitness in clarifying the action of the state in the domain of scientific research, the LOLF reform excited the expression and characteristics of two complementary, but quite different, operators of statistical production. One was a statistical unit inside the Ministry of Higher Education and Research: the Department of Evaluation and Forecasting ('Direction de l'évaluation et de la prospective'), which specialized in labour statistics, educational statistics, econometrics and national statistical surveys. The other was a public interest agency that had pioneered policy-oriented scientometrics in France: the Observatory of Science and Technology ('Observatoire des sciences et des techniques'). The agency reports on science and innovation positioning, analyses data from a variety of sources, for example, the ISI bibliographic database (initially maintained by the Institute for Scientific Information, which was then acquired by Thomson Scientific, now Thomson Reuters, and which is currently known as Web of Knowledge), but also the Organisation for Economic Co-operation and Development (OECD), Eurostat and others. The ideas and tools that characterized the Department of Evaluation and Forecasting revolved around the legacy of national statistics, the professional trajectories of state statisticians and economists, and the practice of large national statistical surveys. In contrast, the Observatory of Science and Technology was explicitly inspired by science and technology studies; a report by notable contributors to the sociology of science (Michel Callon in particular) was what motivated its creation in 1986 (Arvanitis *et al.* 1986; see also Callon 1986c; Barré 2010).

It is true that assessing scientific production through scientometrics matches an idea of the scientist as some sort of an authorship entrepreneur who is functionally preoccupied with positioning and reputation (Pontille 2004; Pontille and Torny 2013). That sounds quite neoliberal, in a way. Producers of scientometric indicators, in particular from the above-mentioned Observatory of Science and Technology, are themselves well aware of the fact that their instruments enter the political arena through their participation in new social and economic evolutions: 'indicators themselves are becoming part of the political discussion and power struggle, and the objects of criticism and discussion to an extent unknown in the old world of national "statistical" indicators' (Lepori *et al.* 2008: 36). A number of social scientists have indeed expressed concerns about the fate of public science in France and spotted in scientometric assessment methods the vectors of some kind of alienation of research, an ideology of competition that plays on benchmarks, incentives and disincentives in order to transform researchers into scientometric capitalists (e.g. Blay 2009).

But it is interesting to note that one of the early perspectives of the Observatory of Science and Technology seemed to favour a political understanding of science, one that would emphasize informed political decision-making and a strategic orientation, one that would seek to forge a motivated 'indication' of research direction and accountability, quite in line with Michel Callon's policy view (Callon 1986c). One can see in the LOLF thread how the scientometric indicators developed by the Observatory of Science and Technology would allow, for example, for a supple monitoring of scientific 'priorities' or 'priority domains' (nanotechnologies and life sciences, for instance), their overlapping nature, their changing contours, and so on – a simple question of keywords in query parameters. In contrast, the type of statistics mastered at the Ministry's Department of Evaluation and Forecasting would require meaningful, neat and homogeneous time series, 'meaningful' meaning in particular not subject to changes in nomenclatures and labels that would follow political moods ('orientations', 'priorities', and so on). Costly questionnaire-based surveys on R&D investment and expenditures in the public and private sectors (a speciality of the Department of Evaluation and Forecasting, used to calculate indicators such as the Gross Domestic Expenditures on R&D, whose elaboration follows prescriptions from the OECD's Frascati Manual) would not allow for this kind of discretional (one may want to say liberal) politics of indication. One can perhaps sense there elements of a statistical tradition inspired by an OECD-driven linear view of innovation and by a much economized view of science (Godin 2005, 2006).

Indicating an economic effect

The LOLF's trial of explicitness was in part about what it meant to quantify scientific production and about who was better equipped to do that. Styles of statistical work were put to the test, all with slightly different views of what quantification, science and also the state were about, and their roles in the economy. Without much surprise, indeed the state's 'role in the economy' was a paramount concern in the semiotic haze, and this touched the role of scientific research, in the form of debate over state-sponsored or state-conducted scientific research and its consequences. Considering science in terms of economic effects is, of course, problematic. The name often put on that problem is 'innovation', a brilliant but obscure concept that conveys, sometimes hesitantly and sometimes explicitly, the idea of translating something from an area called 'science' (laboratories, universities, etc.) to another one called 'the economy' (firms, industry, technological applications, etc.). The thing that undergoes translation (knowledge?) is hard to define, but what counts are the accounting instruments that allow it to be shown that some kind of translation (or 'transfer' as practitioners put it) is going on: patents, revenues, those types of things which are recurrently taken as quantifiable proxies for economic effects (Robson 1993, 1994).

As the implementation of the LOLF was to a great extent a matter of proliferation of words, the notion of 'leverage' (*levier* in French) came to nourish the referential repertoire of the semiotic haze. Let us briefly browse the little quandaries raised by one particular indicator termed 'Leverage effect of incentives aimed at favouring firm creation' ('Effet de levier des moyens incitatifs publics mobilisés en faveur de la création d'entreprises'). The meaning may be unclear for the reader, as it was for the researcher who stumbled upon it and, apparently, a number of field actors. The notion of 'leverage' or 'leverage effect' is metaphorically engaging, prone to imagery and interpretation

('Give me a lever and I shall move the economy'). The expression *'effet de levier'* is often used in French, rather intuitively, to refer to magnifying the force of an initial effort. For a translation into more economic terms, one just has to replace 'force' with 'economic return' and 'initial effort' with 'investment'. In a more technical, financial denotation, the notion of 'leverage' introduces the external character of the initial effort (which is borrowed from or given by an external party) and a subsequent notion of due or indebtedness. The notion can then refer, for example, to a practice of speculative investment of borrowed funds or, in the case examined here, to an estimation of the relationship between initial external funds and final return on investment. Note from the outset that 'the investor' – which I interpret as an imaginary private character who possesses money and is free to put it where profit can be maximized (Ortiz 2011) – is here something like 'the state'. That is indeed an outstanding achievement in terms of the anthropological configuration of the state. It becomes an investment agency (*investissement* is the prevailing world in current French administrative nomenclatures, much preferred to *financement* or to just *budget*).

The indicator titled 'Leverage effect of incentives aimed at favouring firm creation' corresponds to a ratio whose terms are the revenues of high-tech start-up companies on one hand, and the amount of funding received by these companies from state offices for innovation or national incubators on the other. An 'economic effect' here is supposed to mean a contribution to 'growth' or 'value creation' (i.e. making money, in more prosaic and nonetheless empirical terms) by stimulating commercial, risk-taking, entrepreneurial conduct in science-based innovation ventures. And 'of the state' is supposed to signify public funding of these enterprises in the form of some sort of governmental venture capital (Doganova 2012). I say 'supposed to' because the referential chains that will link the indicator to 'the economic effect of the action state' were exposed to a number of trials.

Here is, for example, one notable objection that we found in the archives: the earnings–funding ratio for a firm 'can only be a good indicator if we consider earnings limited to the innovation project' funded by the national incubators; otherwise, an external factor on earnings such as 'favourable exchange rates in exports' could end up being interpreted as a result of actions of the state, which is silly (Muniesa and Linhardt 2011: 562–3). A private company is a private company, and its fate is not determined by the state simply because the state invested some money into some small part of the venture. All or almost all of the statisticians who discussed that indicator (both from the Department of Evaluation and Forecasting and from the Observatory of Science and Technology) critiqued using the annual leverage effect of incentives as a proxy for the economic impact of state-driven innovation policy. It was simply irrelevant. But the indicator stayed, nonetheless. One can always add a disclaimer to an indicator, to adjust its formulation so as to prevent referential chains based on faulty assumptions. It certainly would have been a pity not to introduce some sort of quantitative characterization of the envisioned role of the state: which is the encouragement of business, viable and competitive business.

Was that formulation, the 'leverage effect of incentives', just too good to be dropped? As we have briefly seen, the major problem it carried was not a lack of interest. It was rather a problem of contour. We know from a number of contributions to the political sociology of the formation of the economy (and from Michel Foucault in particular), that this thing, 'the economy', is entirely a construction operated by the state. But we are today in a situation in which the use of quotation marks for 'the economy' is no longer in order. It is, perhaps, for 'the state', as this entity has become an agent whose political function is to encourage the economy through means that are rather meagre, since the identification and efficacy of its action (a public subsidy, a doctoral grant, a university patent, a scientific paper) is conceived of as an intervention into a reality (the economy) that is no longer the state's reality.

Provoking a state of economy

At the heart of economic indication in public administration lie the crafts of the delineation of inputs, outputs and outcomes. Scholarship related to performativity certainly needs to address the force that in this regard has carried and still carries the consultancy literature on 'public value' and its 'unlocking' (e.g. Poister 2003, Osborne and Hutchinson 2004, Cole and Parston 2006). Crafting sound performance indicators and creating the right templates to craft more constitute a prevailing task in this literature and its associated consultancy services. And the distinction between input, output and outcome indicators is an acknowledged, major achievement.

The LOLF Act of 2001 highlighted the importance of accounting for the 'results' (*résultats*) of the state's actions, but was not very explicit about whether this refers to the 'outputs' of such action (i.e. what the state does, its specific products or services), its 'outcomes' (i.e. the effect of these products or services on the reality known as 'the public', 'the nation', 'the economy' or 'society') or both. Subsequent documents and guidelines attempted to clarify this point. The official version ended up being one that established a distinction between indicators for 'final results' (impacts on national reality seen from the viewpoint of 'the citizen', which corresponds to outcomes in standard managerial parlance); 'quality' (products and services, hence outputs, considered in terms of timeliness and the satisfaction of 'the user'); and 'efficiency' (outputs considered in light of their costs, serving, thus, the viewpoint of 'the taxpayer').

Despite being obviously very cogent, at least at first sight, this template did not circulate without adaptations, hesitations, clarifications and interrogations throughout the implementation process. In my view, the most telling issues were about the delimitation of the agency and perimeter of the state, as if this entity was reluctant to enter such a regime of clarification. Scientific research is a combination of activities that are undeniably linked to the state. But the question is how. In the archives examined at the Ministry of Higher Education and Research, some documents display an implicit view of public scientific research as a direct action of the state. Science is produced by researchers who work for national laboratories and state universities. These workers are agents of the state based on payroll, as well as their mandate, so their output is, in a sense, an output of the state. Scientific production (publications, patents, prototypes, seminars, lectures, ideas) is thus some sort of a public product or service. This product or service, it is implied from this viewpoint, can in turn have effects (outcomes) on other types of realities outside the state: for example on the economy (by fostering innovation and competitiveness through some particular means) or on the public (by contributing to public scientific culture through some other particular means). The state does the science and this action has effects on other things. In some other documents, however, science is not done by the state. What the state does is provide means and incentives to a community of practitioners of science. What these practitioners carry out are rather consequences (outcomes?) of the actions of the state, not the actions of the state (outputs?) proper.

Of course, the question 'Was it the state or was it not?' can sound a bit metaphysical, and certainly things can work without settling it at all. But the introduction of indicators certainly served as a call for explicitness: something qualitatively new that was not part of the state beforehand. Calls for a neat distinction of outputs from outcomes generate indeed, in a performative fashion, a whole set of novel concerns, procedures and ideas of what the state is that simply did not exist as such beforehand, in my opinion. Imagine, for example, a position for which the idea of the state would be characterized, precisely, by outputs and outcomes being indistinguishable. This is a position that seems to me to be quite classical on the political identity of the sovereign state and its function in the constitution of reality, a position that is not quite sustainable now, if one is to make the state's action explicit in line with an 'inside/outside', 'cause/effect' template.

I am a researcher at the École des Mines de Paris; I am not a civil servant proper, but I am still on the state's payroll. This book is part of my official job (this paragraph was written during office hours). The book is also listed as a deliverable for a project funded by the European Research Council, which sends money to the École des Mines de Paris. Is this book an output of the action of the state? Is it an outcome? Or is its effect on you an outcome? Imagine now that I apply for some research-based spin-off funding from the state in order to turn the concepts outlined in this book into a profitable start-up company and that, after a few years, I make money from it. Is the money that I make an economic outcome of the action of the state? Or an output? Or perhaps an input, since money that goes into my pocket is money that increases the wealth of an agent of the state? These are ridiculous questions, right? They sound like some sort of a breaching thought experiment, halfway between an ethnomethodological approach to the realization of the state and a silly joke. But it seems that this is a serious thing. Perhaps the semiotic urge that accompanied the reform examined here did not aim to clarify such questions. However, it definitely contributed to setting up a frame in which they could (and should) be asked, albeit clumsily. But then again, almost everything starts clumsily. The fact is, now I am asking you these strange questions.

There is certainly a sense in the potential answers that I may just take my book and my revenues and do my business as I see fit, that I may use all of this to increase my reputation in a competitive, volatile market for academic careers. I may enter into new valuation networks, perhaps also capitalization networks, that concern me personally and the state may just go away, fade out, become nothing – at least nothing that is present in the fact that I have written a book that you are now reading. Perhaps, as the result of this drive towards the economic signification of its action, the state will simply tell us that it does not exist. What exists is a market for research and researchers – and for books.

But another interpretation of this thought experiment could go in an entirely different direction. We could agree on the fact that, indeed, this book (and possibly also its economic fate) constitute some sort of a public service, something that emerges out of the combination of, on the one hand, the independent perception by its author of the timeliness of the topics covered and, on the other hand, the generosity of France and Europe in channelling scientific force. This constitutes an action of the state, though perhaps not exactly an economic one.

Tentative conclusion

A cogent appraisal of the spirit of contemporary capitalism and its problems calls, I believe, for renewed attention to the performative. Business schools, consultancy firms, corporations, investment banks, start-up companies, market research agencies, public administrations and other sites of business life are characterized by the presence of habits, idioms and apparatuses that constitute a significant part of the reality of business. These include techniques for the simulation of business situations, methods for the explanation of business problems, instruments for the valuation of business endeavours, and tools for the presentation of business outcomes. But simulation, explanation, valuation and presentation are not only about accounting for external states of affair. They are, at least in part, about moulding, enacting, provoking and effecting the business realities they signify. In short, they are performative. From a social-scientific perspective, this means that an examination of today's business culture (an examination whose urgency now seems justified by the great bearings that this culture has on our world and our lives) requires critical attention to the intricacies of performativity.

Critical attention to the intricacies of performativity in economic matters in general and in business life in particular involves, in turn, taking into account the four problems that I have attempted to explain in the previous pages: description, simulacrum, explicitness and provocation. First, ordinary business activities are activities of description, as business realities consist of nothing more and nothing less than the piling up and public display of layers of documents, presentations, diagrams and formulas that designate business objects and, in so doing, grant them with agency. A materialist, semiotic scrutiny of how descriptions organize things becomes crucial to understanding how business reality comes about. Second, economic life is cluttered with simulacra, situations of simulation that often plunge commentators and practitioners alike into some sort of epistemic and moral discomfort, but which ultimately constitute the very vehicle for the realization of business, with realization understood in both the sense of becoming actual and becoming meaningful. Considering the simulacrum as a technique of effectuation becomes a critical ingredient of the social studies of business. Third, economic life is the locus *par excellence* of reflexivity and escalation in assessment and verification, but explicating economic things translates into more uncertainty, more indeterminacy and the generation of more things to be made explicit. Analysing economic organizing in the terms of trials of explicitness becomes a stimulating instrument for the observation of tensions and struggles over business power. Finally, one distinctive feature of the demonstration of economic problems in both business training and actual business practice is its particular form of artificially generated, highly visual, staged, measured form of realism. Recognizing the particular blend of provoked realism that animates business culture becomes a fine entry point for the understanding of the empirical philosophy of the conduct of business.

But is performativity wrong, one may ask? Is there something dodgy or unsafe going on with all of these performative things happening? Some critics of business culture, capitalism and economic drive at large may put forward, in a fairly modernistic tradition of thought, the need to replace lies, gesticulations and decoys in the display of business by a more authentic, truthful and transparent vision of economic reality. They are not at ease with performativity. But performativity is not about leading astray, it is about realizing – and, I want to add, so is critique. Critique in the midst of the performative turn is (or should be) thus best understood as experimental critique.

What I mean by that, in particular, is that effective forms of critical appreciation engage with the four features of the performative that I have emphasized in these pages. Judicious and judgemental accounts of economic situations and of business endeavours are descriptions. They provide in this sense new texts, new documents that add to the existing and that potentially organize what they refer to in new ways. They are critical (as opposed to indiscriminating and unsuspecting descriptions) in the sense that what they describe is a problem: an inherent prejudice, an unforeseen damage, a justificatory contradiction. As soon as these accounts are tactically positioned and released, they grant their authors and supporters the capacity to experiment with articulation. Take, for example, a complex financial product and how its critical description can translate into juristic language, accountancy methodologies, governance procedures or due process. Take, for example, a performance indicator and how its critical description can translate into managerial and counter-managerial instruments, into new semiotic keys of indication.

Experimental critique also partakes of the simulacrum. In order to realize a problem (which is what critique is about) the critical statement enters the crafts of performative demonstration. To realize means to play, to effect. Even critique conforming to the habits of scholarly denouncement proceeds in such a manner, although it is limited to the classic setting of the seminar room. Expanding the sites and methods of the simulation of reality and its consequences definitely enhances the efficacy of critique. Think, for instance, of how marginal economic experiments (radical ecological ventures, small-scale communal arrangements, extreme speculative investments) can be magnified and stand as relevant cases and thus relevant points of reference in the realization of what is happening: they may not have wider-reaching consequences, as some would put it, but in fact they do something since they help realize something.

The problem of explicitness also affects the experimental critique of business assemblages and of economic things. In order to move slightly away from the habits of scholarly negativity and enter into the polity with a more propositional attitude, the critical stance has to cope with the task of making itself explicit. And this is about taking risks, because facing trials of explicitness means exposure to error and contradiction, to consequences and externalities, and hence to further criticism, objection and contestation. Explicitness fuels debate. And this is perhaps another way of considering the transition between a critical stance and a political one. When the critique of reality is done in a way in which an articulated alternative is required, being explicit about that alternative contributes to the opening up of a space of deliberation, a space of encounter with parties at stake, a space eventually for experimental implementation – and this can be the case in domains as crucial as the critique of financial expansion or marketing extension.

As for provocation, it is, of course, not the task of critical approaches to business life to be provocative in the sense of being bold and confrontational. Experimental critique is provocative in the very sense that it is an experimental event. It is an event that creates a situation to which and for which participants have to respond – and participants include all experimental researchers and affected parties alike. Provocative methodologies are not methodologies of resistance to reality – to economic reality, in the case considered here. Quite the contrary, the provocative critique of the economy envisages a reality that is not the same once the critique has happened.

How this differs from alternative views on what critique should be about remains an open question. The point is definitely not to spot the one best definition of critique and to see who endorses it and who does not. We are, as I write, in the early 2010s, and there certainly are a lot of things to be critical about, in many different ways. If being critical means saying that things are bad (which is one way critique is predominantly understood in the social sciences today), then it looks like there is plenty of choice in our dubious economic world (depending of course on the 'we' who talks). If it means considering truth from all possible angles (in the often forgotten philosophical sense of the world), it is also clear that there is still a plethora of things to be studied about the connections and contradictions that govern our thought (also with a caveat on 'our'). If it means setting κρίσις (*krísis*) in motion (instituting a distinction, drawing a separation or, more prosaically, just changing things), then we surely need to acknowledge the countless interventions that purposefully aim at marking our economic reality (and our political deictics too). The point of the idea of experimental critique is to add to this but a nuance: that, in all cases, the performative condition of the critical undertaking should not be taken as some sort of demoralizing deterrence, but rather as part of its deliberate methodology. And the how and the where remains also an open question – definitely not something these pages could settle.

Bibliography

Abraham, Y.-M. and Sardais, C. (2008) 'Pour une autre théorie de la decision: retour sur la faillite de la banque Barings (et de sa hiérarchie…)', *Gérer et Comprendre*, 92: 4–22.
Aggeri, F. and Labatut, J. (2010) 'La gestion au prisme de ses instruments: une analyse généalogique des approches théoriques fondées sur les instruments de gestion', *Finance Contrôle Stratégie*, 13(3): 5–37.
Aglietta, M. (1976) *Régulation et Crises du Capitalisme: l'expérience des États-Unis*, Paris: Calman-Lévy.
——(1995) *Macroéconomie Financière*, Paris: La Découverte.
Agnew, J.-C. (1986) *Worlds Apart: the market and the theater in Anglo-American thought, 1550–1750*, Cambridge: Cambridge University Press.
Alvesson, M., Willmott, H. and Bridgman, T. (eds) (2009) *The Oxford Handbook of Critical Management Studies*, Oxford: Oxford University Press.
Amin, A. and Thrift, N. (eds) (2004) *The Blackwell Cultural Economy Reader*, Oxford: Blackwell.
Andrews, K.R. (ed.) (1953) *The Case Method of Teaching Human Relations and Administration*, Cambridge (Massachusetts): Harvard University Press.
Anteby, M. (2013) *Manufacturing Morals: the values of silence in business school education*, Chicago: The University of Chicago Press.
Araujo, L. (2007) 'Markets, market-making and marketing', *Marketing Theory*, 7(3): 211–26.
Araujo, L., Finch, J. and Kjellberg, H. (eds) (2010) *Reconnecting Marketing to Markets*, Oxford: Oxford University Press.
Armatte, M. (2010) *La Science Économique comme Ingénierie: quantification et modélisation*, Paris: Presses des Mines.
Arnaboldi, M. and Azzone, G. (2010) 'Constructing performance measurement in the public sector', *Critical Perspectives on Accounting*, 21(4): 266–82.
Arvanitis, R., Callon, M. and Latour, B. (1986) *Évaluation des Politiques Publiques de la Recherche et de la Technologie: analyse des programmes nationaux de la recherche*, Paris: La Documentation Française.

Assmann, J. (1992) 'Inscriptional violence and the art of cursing: a study of performative writing', *Stanford Literary Review*, 9(1): 43–65.

Austin, J.L. (1962) *How to Do Things with Words*, Oxford: Clarendon Press.

Ayache, E. (2010) *The Blank Swan: the end of probability*, Chichester: John Wiley & Sons.

Babb, S. (2004) *Managing Mexico: economists from nationalism to neoliberalism*, Princeton (New Jersey): Princeton University Press.

Baden-Fuller, C. and Morgan, M.S. (2010) 'Business models as models', *Long Range Planning*, 43(2–3): 156–71.

Barilari, A. and Bouvier, M. (2007) *La LOLF et la Nouvelle Gouvernance Financière de l'État*, Paris: LFDJ.

Barnes, L.B., Christensen, C.R. and Hansen, A.J. (1994) *Teaching and the Case Method*, Boston: Harvard Business School Press.

Barré, R. (2010) '"De l'arbitraire à l'arbitrage": les indicateurs de S& t en débat', in M. Akrich, Y. Barthe, F. Muniesa and P. Mustar (eds), *Débordements: mélanges offerts à Michel Callon*, Paris: Presses des Mines.

Barry, A. (2001) *Political Machines: governing a technological society*, London: The Athlone Press.

——(2002) 'The anti-political economy', *Economy and Society*, 31(2): 268–84.

Barry, A., Osborne, T. and Rose, N. (eds) (1996) *Foucault and Political Reason: liberalism, neo-liberalism, and rationalities of government*, London: Routledge.

Baudrillard, J. (1981) *Simulacres et Simulation*, Paris: Galilée.

——(1994) *Simulacra and Simulation*, Ann Arbor: The University of Michigan Press.

Beaudoin, V. (2008) 'PowerPoint: le lit de Procuste revisité', *Social Science Information*, 47(3): 371–90.

Beck, U., Giddens, A. and Lash, S. (1994) *Reflexive Modernization: politics, tradition and aesthetics in the modern social order*, Cambridge: Polity Press.

Bell, V. (ed.) (1999) *Performativity and Belonging*, London: Sage.

——(2007) *Culture and Performance: the challenge of ethics, politics and feminist theory*, Oxford: Berg.

Benveniste, É. (1969) *Le Vocabulaire des Institutions Indo-Européennes*, Paris: Éditions de Minuit.

——(1973) *Indo-European Language and Society*, London: Faber and Faber.

Beunza, D. and Stark, D. (2004) 'Tools of the trade: the socio-technology of arbitrage in a Wall Street trading room', *Industrial and Corporate Change*, 13(2): 369–400.

——(2012) 'From dissonance to resonance: cognitive interdependence in quantitative finance', *Economy and Society*, 41(3): 383–417.

Bevan, G. and Hood, C. (2006) 'What's measured is what matters: targets and gaming in the English public health care system', *Public Administration*, 84(3): 517–38.

Bezes, P. (2005) 'L'État et les savoirs managériaux: essor et développement de la gestion publique en France', in F. Lacasse and P.-E. Verrier (eds), *Trente*

Ans de Réforme de l'État: expériences françaises et étrangères, stratégies et bilans, Paris: Dunod.

——(2008) 'Le tournant néomanagérial de l'administration française', in O. Borraz and V. Guiraudon (eds), *Politiques Publiques: 1, la France dans la gouvernance européenne*, Paris: Presses de Sciences Po.

——(2009) *Réinventer l'État: les réformes de l'administration française (1962–2008)*, Paris: PUF.

——(2012) 'État, experts et savoirs néo-managériaux: les producteurs et diffuseurs du New Public Management en France depuis les années 1970', *Actes de la Recherche en Sciences Sociales*, 193: 16–37.

Biehl-Missal, B. (2011) 'Business is show business: management presentations as performance', *Journal of Management Studies*, 48(3): 619–45.

Black, F. (1971a) 'Toward a fully automated stock exchange', *Financial Analysts Journal*, 27(4): 28–35, 44.

——(1971b) 'Toward a fully automated stock exchange II', *Financial Analysts Journal*, 27(6): 25–8, 86–7.

Blass, T. (2004) *The Man who Shocked the World: the life and legacy of Stanley Milgram*, New York: Basic Books.

Blay, L. (2009) 'L'évaluation par indicateurs dans la vie scientifique: choix politique et fin de la connaissance', *Cités*, 37: 15–25.

Bockman, J. and Eyal, G. (2002) 'Eastern Europe as a laboratory for economic knowledge: the transnational roots of neoliberalism', *American Journal of Sociology*, 108(2): 310–52.

Boltanski, L. and Chiapello, È. (1999) *Le Nouvel Esprit du Capitalisme*, Paris: Gallimard.

——(2006) *The New Spirit of Capitalism*, London: Verso.

Bourdieu, P. (1981) 'Men and machines', in K.D. Knorr Cetina and A.V. Cicourel (eds), *Advances in Social Theory and Methodology: toward an integration of micro- and macro-sociologies*, Boston: Routledge and Kegan Paul.

——(1997) 'Le champ économique', *Actes de la Recherche en Sciences Sociales*, 119: 48–66.

——(2000) *Les Structures Sociales de l'Économie*, Paris: Seuil.

——(2005) *The Social Structures of the Economy*, Cambridge: Polity Press.

Boyer, R. (1990) *The Regulation School: a critical introduction*, New York: Columbia University Press.

Brannigan, A. (2004) *The Rise and Fall of Social Psychology: an iconoclast's guide to the use and misuse of the experimental method*, Berlin: Walter de Gruyter.

Breslau, D. (2005) 'Economics invents the economy: mathematics, statistics, and models in the work of Irving Fisher and Wesley Mitchell', *Theory and Society*, 32(3): 379–411.

Breslau, D. and Yonay, Y. (1999) 'Beyond metaphor: mathematical models in economics as empirical research', *Science in Context*, 12(2): 317–32.

Bibliography

Brown, A.D. (2005) 'Making sense of the collapse of Barings Bank', *Human Relations*, 58(12): 1579–604.

Brügger, U. (2000) 'Speculating: work in financial markets', in H. Kalthoff, R. Rottenburg and H.-J. Wagener (eds), *Facts and Figures: economic representations and practices*, Marburg: Metropolis-Verlag.

Brunetière, J.-R. (2006) 'Les indicateurs de la loi organique relative aux lois de finances (LOLF): une occasion de débat démocratique?' *Revue Française d'Administration Publique*, 117: 95–111.

Bruno, I. and Didier, E. (2013) *Benchmarking: l'État sous pression statistique*, Paris: La Découverte.

Buchler, J. (ed.) (1955) *Philosophical Writings of Peirce*, New York: Dover Publications.

Burchell, G., Gordon, C. and Miller, P. (eds) (1991) *The Foucault Effect: studies in governmentality*, Chicago: The University of Chicago Press.

Butler, J. (1993) *Bodies that Matter: on the discursive limits of 'sex'*, London: Routledge.

Çalışkan, K. (2010) *Market Threads: how cotton farmers and traders create a global commodity*, Princeton (New Jersey): Princeton University Press.

Çalışkan, K. and Callon, M. (2009) 'Economization, part 1: shifting attention from the economy towards processes of economization', *Economy and Society*, 38(3): 369–98.

——(2010) 'Economization, part 2: a research programme for the study of markets', *Economy and Society*, 39(1): 1–32.

Callon, M. (1976) 'L'opération de traduction comme relation symbolique', in C. Gruson (ed.), *Incidence des Rapports Sociaux sur le Développement Scientifique et Technique*, Paris: CORDES.

——(1986a) 'Éléments pour une sociologie de la traduction: la domestication des coquilles Saint-Jacques et des marins-pêcheurs dans la baie de Saint-Brieuc', *L'Année Sociologique*, 36: 169–208.

——(1986b) 'Some elements of a sociology of translation: domestication of the scallops and the fishermen of St. Brieuc Bay', in J. Law (ed.), *Power, Action and Belief: a new sociology of knowledge?* London: Routledge.

——(1986c) 'Les indicateurs des sciences et des techniques', *Recherche Technologique*, 1: 41–51.

——(1998) 'Introduction: the embeddedness of economic markets in economics', in M. Callon (ed.), *The Laws of the Markets*, Oxford: Blackwell.

——(1999) 'Actor-network theory: the market test', in J. Law and J. Hassard (eds), *Actor Network Theory and After*, Oxford: Blackwell.

——(2007) 'What does it mean to say that economics is performative?', in D. MacKenzie, F. Muniesa and L. Siu (eds), *Do Economists Make Markets? On the performativity of economics*, Princeton (New Jersey): Princeton University Press.

——(2009) 'Civilizing markets: carbon trading between in vitro and in vivo experiments', *Accounting, Organizations and Society*, 34(3–4): 535–48.

Callon, M. and Latour, B. (1981) 'Unscrewing the big Leviathan: how actors macrostructure reality and how sociologists help them to do so', in K.D. Knorr Cetina and A.V. Cicourel (eds), *Advances in Social Theory and Methodology: toward an integration of micro- and macro-sociologies*, Boston: Routledge and Kegan Paul.

——(1997) 'Tu ne calculeras pas! Comment symétriser le don et le capital', *Revue du MAUSS*, 9(1): 45–70.

Callon, M. and Muniesa, F. (2005) 'Economic markets as calculative collective devices', *Organization Studies*, 26(8): 1229–50.

Callon, M., Méadel, C. and Rabeharisoa, V. (2000) 'L'économie des qualités', *Politix*, 52: 211–39.

——(2002) 'The economy of qualities', *Economy and Society*, 31(2): 194–217.

Callon, M., Millo, Y. and Muniesa, F. (eds) (2007) *Market Devices*, Oxford: Blackwell.

Carrier, J.G. and Miller, D. (eds) (1998) *Virtualism: a new political economy*, Oxford: Berg.

Cartwright, N. (1999) *The Dappled World: a study of the boundaries of science*, Cambridge: Cambridge University Press.

Chapman, C.S. (ed.) (2005) *Controlling Strategy: management, accounting, and performance measurement*, Oxford: Oxford University Press.

Chiapello, È. (2007) 'Accounting and the birth of the notion of capitalism', *Critical Perspectives on Accounting*, 18(3): 263–96.

Chiapello, È. and Gilbert, P. (2013) *Sociologie des Outils de Gestion: introduction à l'analyse sociale de l'instrumentation de gestion*, Paris: La Découverte.

Christensen, C.R. (1981) *Teaching by the Case Method*, Boston: Harvard Business School, Division of Research.

Christensen, C.R., Garvin, D.A. and Sweet, A. (eds) (1991) *Education for Judgment: the artistry of discussion leadership*, Boston: Harvard Business School Press.

Clark, T. (2008) 'Performing the organization: organization theatre and imaginative life as physical presence', in D. Barry and H. Hansen (eds), *The SAGE Handbook of New Approaches in Management and Organization*, London: Sage.

Cochoy, F. (1999) *Une Histoire du Marketing: discipliner l'économie de marché*, Paris: La Découverte.

——(2002) *Une Sociologie du Packaging ou l'Âne de Buridan Face au Marché*, Paris: PUF.

Colander, D. (2008) 'Review: Do Economists Make Markets? On the performativity of economics', *Journal of Economic Literature*, 46(3): 720–4.

Cole, M. and Parston, G. (2006) *Unlocking Public Value: a new model for achieving high performance in public service organizations*, Hoboken (New Jersey): Wiley.

Contardo, I. and Wensley, R. (2004) 'The Harvard Business School story: avoiding knowledge by being relevant', *Organization*, 11(2): 211–31.

Bibliography

Cooren, F. (2000) *The Organizing Property of Communication*, Amsterdam: John Benjamins.

——(2004) 'Textual agency: how texts do things in organizational settings', *Organization*, 11(3): 373–93.

——(2010) *Action and Agency in Dialogue: passion, incarnation and ventriloquism*, Amsterdam: John Benjamins.

Cooren, F., Taylor, J.R. and Van Every, E.J. (eds) (2006) *Communication as Organizing: empirical and theoretical explorations in the dynamic of text and conversation*, Mahwah (New Jersey): Lawrence Erlbaum Associates.

Copeland, M.T. (1958) *And Mark an Era: the story of the Harvard Business School*, Boston: Little, Brown and Co.

Corbett, A. (2010) 'Public management policymaking in France: legislating the Organic Law on Laws of Finance (LOLF), 1998–2001', *Governance*, 23 (2): 225–49.

Coriat, B. (1979) *L'Atelier et le Chronomètre: essai sur le taylorisme, le fordisme et la production de masse*, Paris: Christian Bourgeois.

Cournot, A. (1838) *Recherches sur les Principes Mathématiques de la Théorie des Richesses*, Paris: Hachette.

Crosby, A.W. (1997) *The Measure of Reality: quantification and Western society, 1250–1600*, Cambridge: Cambridge University Press.

Cruikshank, J.L. (1987) *A Delicate Experiment: the Harvard Business School, 1908–1945*, Boston: Harvard Business School Press.

Cytermann, J.-R. (2006) 'L'architecture de la Loi organique relative aux lois de finances (LOLF) dans les domaines de l'éducation et de la recherche: choix politiques ou choix techniques?', *Revue Française d'Administration Publique*, 117: 85–94.

Czarniawska, B. (1997) *Narrating the Organization: dramas of institutional identity*, Chicago: The University of Chicago Press.

Czarniawska, B. and Hernes, T. (eds) (2005) *Actor-Network Theory and Organizing*, Malmö: Liber & Copenhagen Business School Press.

Daston, L. and Galison, P. (2007) *Objectivity*, New York: Zone Books.

Datar, S.M., Garvin, D.A. and Cullen, P. (2010) *Rethinking the MBA: business education at a crossroads*, Boston: Harvard Business Press.

Davies, W. (2009) 'The making of neo-liberalism', *Renewal*, 17(4): 88–92.

De Goede, M. (2005) *Virtue, Fortune, and Faith: a genealogy of finance*, Minneapolis (Minnesota): University of Minnesota Press.

Deleuze, G. (1966) *Le Bergsonisme*, Paris: PUF.

——(1968a) *Différence et Répétition*, Paris: PUF.

——(1968b) *Spinoza et le Problème de l'Expression*, Paris: Éditions de Minuit.

——(1969) *Logique du Sens*, Paris: Éditions de Minuit.

——(1988a) *Le Pli: Leibniz et le baroque*, Paris: Éditions de Minuit.

——(1988b) *Bergsonism*, New York: Zone Books.

——(1990a) *Logic of Sense*, New York: Columbia University Press.

——(1990b) *Expressionism in Philosophy: Spinoza*, New York: Zone Books.
——(1992) 'L'épuisé', afterword in S. Beckett, *Quad et Autres Pieces pour la Télévision*, Paris: Éditions de Minuit.
——(1993) *The Fold: Leibniz and the baroque*, Minneapolis (Minnesota): University of Minnesota Press.
——(1994) *Difference and Repetition*, New York: Columbia University Press.
——(1995) 'The exhausted', *SubStance*, 24(3): 3–28.
Deleuze, G. and Guattari, F. (1972) *L'Anti-Œdipe*, Paris: Éditions de Minuit.
——(1980) *Mille Plateaux*, Paris: Éditions de Minuit.
——(1983) *Anti-Oedipus: capitalism and schizophrenia*, Minneapolis (Minnesota): University of Minnesota Press.
——(1987) *A Thousand Plateaux: capitalism and schizophrenia*, Minneapolis (Minnesota): University of Minnesota Press.
Demeulenaere, P. (1996) *Homo Œconomicus: enquête sur la constitution d'un paradigme*, Paris: PUF.
Denis, J. and Pontille, D. (2010a) 'Performativité de l'écrit et travail de maintenance', *Réseaux*, 163: 105–30.
——(2010b) 'Placing subway signs: practical properties of signs at work', *Visual Communication*, 9(4): 441–62.
——(2010c) 'The graphical performation of a public space: the subway signs and their scripts', in G. Sonda, C. Coletta and F. Gabbi (eds), *Urban Plots, Organizing Cities*, Farnham: Ashgate.
Derrida, J. (1967) *De la Grammatologie*, Paris: Éditions de Minuit.
Descola, P. (1996) *In the Society of Nature: a native ecology in Amazonia*, Cambridge: Cambridge University Press.
——(2005) *Par-delà Nature et Culture*, Paris: Gallimard.
——(2013) *Beyond Nature and Culture*, Chicago: The University of Chicago Press.
Despret, V. (2004a) *Hans, le Cheval Qui Savait Compter*, Paris: Les Empêcheurs de Penser en Rond.
——(2004b) 'The body we care for: figures of anthropo-zoo-genesis', *Body & Society*, 10(2–3): 111–34.
Desrosières, A. (1993) *La Politique des Grands Nombres: histoire de la raison statistique*, Paris: La Découverte.
——(1998) *The Politics of Large Numbers: a history of statistical reasoning*, Cambridge (Massachusetts): Harvard University Press.
——(2003a) 'Historiciser l'action publique: l'État, le marché et les statistiques', in P. Laborier and D. Trom (eds), *Historicités de l'Action Publique*, Paris: PUF.
——(2003b) 'Managing the economy', in T.M. Porter and D. Ross (eds), *The Cambridge History of Science, Volume 7: the modern social sciences*, Cambridge: Cambridge University Press.
Dewey, J. (1916) *Democracy and Education: an introduction to the philosophy of education*, New York: Macmillan.
——(1939) *Theory of Valuation*, Chicago: The University of Chicago Press.

—— (1946) 'Peirce's theory of linguistic signs, thought, and meaning', *The Journal of Philosophy*, 43(4): 85–95.

Dewing, A.S. (1903) *Introduction to the History of Modern Philosophy*, Philadelphia: J.B. Lippincott Company.

—— (1910) *Life as Reality: a philosophical essay*, New York: Longmans, Green & Co.

—— (1920) *The Financial Policy of Corporations*, New York: The Ronald Press.

—— (1926) *The Financial Policy of Corporations*, revised edn, New York: The Ronald Press.

—— (1927) 'An introduction to the use of cases', in C.E. Fraser, *Problems in Finance*, Chicago: A.W. Shaw Company.

—— (1931) 'An introduction to the use of cases', in C.E. Fraser (ed.), *The Case Method of Instruction: a related series of articles*, New York: McGraw-Hill.

—— (1954) 'An introduction to the use of cases', in M.P. McNair (ed.), *The Case Method at the Harvard Business School: papers by present and past members of the faculty and staff*, New York: McGraw-Hill.

Dezalay, Y. and Garth, B.G. (2002) *The Internationalization of Palace Wars: lawyers, economists, and the contest to transform Latin American states*, Chicago: The University of Chicago Press.

Doganova, L. (2012) *Valoriser la Science: les partenariats des start-up technologiques*, Paris: Presses des Mines.

Doganova, L. and Eyquem-Renault, M. (2009) 'What do business models do? Innovation devices in technology entrepreneurship', *Research Policy*, 38(10): 1559–70.

Domowitz, I. (1990) 'The mechanics of automated trade execution systems', *Journal of Financial Intermediation*, 1(2): 167–94.

—— (1992) 'Automating the price discovery process: some international comparisons and regulatory implications', *Journal of Financial Services Research*, 6(4): 305–26.

—— (1993) 'A taxonomy of automated trade execution systems', *Journal of International Money and Finance*, 12(6): 607–31.

Donham, W.B. (1922) 'Teaching by the case system', *American Economic Review*, 12(1): 53–65.

Dosse, F. (1995) *L'Empire du Sens: l'humanisation des sciences humaines*, Paris: La Découverte.

—— (1999) *Empire of Meaning: the humanization of the social sciences*, Minneapolis (Minnesota): University of Minnesota Press.

Drummond, H. (2003) 'Did Nick Leeson have an accomplice? The role of information technology in the collapse of Barings Bank', *Journal of Information Technology*, 18(2): 93–101.

Du Gay, P. (2000) *In Praise of Bureaucracy: Weber, organization, ethics*, London: Sage.

——(2004) 'Against 'Enterprise' (but not against 'enterprise', for that would make no sense)', *Organization*, 11(1): 37–57.
Du Gay, P. and Morgan, G. (eds) (2013) *New Spirits of Capitalism? Crises, justifications, and dynamics*, Oxford: Oxford University Press.
Du Gay, P. and Pryke, M. (eds) (2002) *Cultural Economy: cultural analysis and commercial life*, London: Sage.
Dubois, D. (2000) 'Categories as acts of meaning: the case of categories in olfaction and audition', *Cognitive Science Quarterly*, 1(1): 35–68.
——(2006) 'Des catégories d'odorants à la sémantique des odeurs: une approche cognitive de l'olfaction', *Terrain*, 47: 89–106.
Dumez, H. and Jeunemaître, A. (1998) 'The unlikely encounter between economics and a market: the case of the cement industry', in M. Callon (ed.), *The Laws of the Markets*, Oxford: Blackwell.
Dumont, L. (1983) *Essais sur l'Individualisme: une perspective anthropologique sur l'idéologie moderne*, Paris: Le Seuil.
——(1986) *Essays on Individualism: modern ideology in anthropological perspective*, Chicago: The University of Chicago Press.
Dupuy, J.-P. (1982) *Ordres et Désordres: enquête sur un nouveau paradigme*, Paris: Seuil.
——(1992a) *Le Sacrifice et l'Envie: le libéralisme aux prises avec la justice sociale*, Paris: Grasset.
——(1992b) *Introduction aux Sciences Sociales: logique des phénomènes collectifs*, Paris: Ellipses.
——(1994) *Aux Origines des Sciences Cognitives*, Paris: La Découverte.
——(2000) *The Mechanization of the Mind: on the origins of cognitive science*, Princeton (New Jersey): Princeton University Press.
Elyachar, J. (2005) *Markets of Dispossession: NGOs, economic development, and the state in Cairo*, Durham (North Carolina): Duke University Press.
Engelen, E., Ertürk, I., Froud, J., Johal, S., Leaver, A., Moran, M., Nilsson, A. and Williams, K. (2011) *After the Great Complacence: financial crisis and the politics of reform*, Oxford: Oxford University Press.
Evans, R.J. (1997) 'Soothsaying or science? Falsification, uncertainty and social change in macroeconometric modelling', *Social Studies of Science*, 27 (3): 395–438.
——(1999a) 'Economic models and policy advice: theory choice or moral choice?' *Science in Context*, 12(2): 351–76.
——(1999b) *Macroeconomic Forecasting: a sociological appraisal*, London: Routledge.
Eyraud, C., El Miri, M. and Perez, P. (2011) 'Les enjeux de quantification dans la LOLF: le cas de l'enseignement supérieur', *Revue Française de Socio-Économie*, 7: 147–68.
Feldman, M.S. (2003) 'A performative perspective on stability and change in organizational routines', *Industrial and Corporate Change*, 12(4): 727–52.

Ferber, M.A. and Nelson, J.A. (eds) (1993) *Beyond Economic Man: feminist theory and economics*, Chicago: The University of Chicago Press.

Fisher, I. (1907) *The Rate of Interest: its nature, determination and relation to economic phenomena*, New York: Macmillan.

Fligstein, N. (1990) *The Transformation of Corporate Control*, Cambridge (Massachusetts): Harvard University Press.

Forman, J. and Rymer, J. (1999) 'The genre system of the Harvard case method', *Journal of Business and Technical Communication*, 13(4): 373–400.

Foucault, M. (1964) 'La prose d'Actéon', *La Nouvelle Revue Française*, 135: 444–59.

——(1970) 'Theatrum philosophicum', *Critique*, 282: 885–908.

——(2001) *L'Herméneutique du Sujet: cours au Collège de France, 1981–1982*, Paris: Gallimard and Seuil.

——(2004a) *Sécurité, Territoire, Population: cours au Collège de France, 1977–1978*, Paris: Gallimard and Seuil.

——(2004b) *Naissance de la Biopolitique: cours au Collège de France, 1978–1979*, Paris: Gallimard and Seuil.

——(2005) *The Hermeneutics of the Subject: lectures at the College de France, 1981–1982*, Basingstoke: Palgrave Macmillan.

——(2007) *Security, Territory, Population: lectures at the College de France, 1977–1978*, Basingstoke: Palgrave Macmillan.

——(2008) *The Birth of Biopolitics: lectures at the College de France, 1978–1979*, Basingstoke: Palgrave Macmillan.

——(2011) *Leçons sur la Volonté de Savoir: cours au Collège de France, 1970–1971*, Paris: Gallimard and Seuil.

Fourcade, M. (2007) 'Theories of markets and theories of society', *American Behavioral Scientist*, 50(8): 1015–34.

——(2009) *Economists and Societies: discipline and profession in the United States, Britain, and France, 1890s to 1990s*, Princeton (New Jersey): Princeton University Press.

Fournier, V. and Grey, C. (2000) 'At the critical moment: conditions and prospects for critical management studies', *Human Relations*, 53(1): 7–32.

Fraser, C.E. (1927) *Problems in Finance*, Chicago: A.W. Shaw Company.

——(1928) 'Growth of the case system in finance', *Ex Libris*, 3(3): 4–6.

——(ed.) (1931) *The Case Method of Instruction: a related series of articles*, New York: McGraw-Hill.

Friedman, D. and Rust, J. (eds) (1993) *The Double Auction Market: institutions, theories, and evidence*, Reading (Massachusetts): Addison-Wesley.

Froud, J., Johal, S., Leaver, A. and Williams, K. (2006) *Financialization and Strategy: narrative and numbers*, London: Routledge.

Gaglio, G. (2009) 'Faire des présentations, c'est travailler, mais comment? Diapositives numériques et chaîne d'activités dans des services marketing', *Activités*, 6(1): 111–38.

Galison, P. (1997) *Image and Logic: a material culture of microphysics*, Chicago: The University of Chicago Press.

Garcia, M.-F. (1986) 'La construction sociale d'un marché parfait: le marché au cadran de Fontaines-en-Sologne', *Actes de la Recherche en Sciences Sociales*, 65: 2–13.

Garcia-Parpet, M.-F. (2007) 'The social construction of a perfect market: the strawberry auction at Fontaines-en-Sologne', in D. MacKenzie, F. Muniesa and L. Siu (eds), *Do Economists Make Markets? On the performativity of economics*, Princeton (New Jersey): Princeton University Press.

Garfinkel, H. (1967) *Studies in Ethnomethodology*, Englewood Cliffs (New Jersey): Prentice-Hall.

Garvin, D.A. (2003) 'Making the case: professional education for the world of practice', *Harvard Magazine*, 106(1): 56–65, 107.

Gerber, D.J. (2010) *Global Competition: law, markets, and globalization*, Oxford: Oxford University Press.

Gherardi, S. and Strati, A. (2012), *Learning and Knowing In Practice-Based Studies*, Cheltenham: Edward Elgar Publishing.

Gibson-Graham, J.K. (1996) *The End of Capitalism (As We Knew It): a feminist critique of political economy*, Oxford: Blackwell.

Giraudeau, M. (2008) 'The drafts of strategy: opening up plans and their uses', *Long Range Planning*, 41(3): 291–308.

——(2012) 'Remembering the future: entrepreneurship guidebooks in the US, from meditation to method (1945–75)', *Foucault Studies*, 13: 40–66.

Godelier, M. (1965) 'Objets et méthodes de l'anthropologie économique', *L'Homme*, 5(2): 32–91.

——(1990) 'La théorie de la transition chez Marx', *Sociologie et Sociétés*, 22(1): 53–81.

Godin, B. (2003) 'The emergence of S&T indicators: why did governments supplement statistics with indicators?' *Research Policy*, 32(4): 679–91.

——(2004) 'The obsession for competitiveness and its impact on statistics: the construction of high-technology indicators', *Research Policy*, 33(8): 1217–29.

——(2005) *Measurement and Statistics on Science and Technology: 1920 to the present*, London: Routledge.

——(2006) 'The linear model of innovation: the historical construction of an analytical framework', *Science, Technology & Human Values*, 31(6): 639–67.

——(2007) 'Science, accounting and statistics: the input-output framework', *Research Policy*, 36(9): 1388–403.

Goffman, E. (1959) *The Presentation of Self in Everyday Life*, Garden City (New York): Anchor Books.

Goswami, M. (2004) *Producing India: from colonial economy to national space*, Chicago: The University of Chicago Press.

Gould, K.A., Pellow, D.N. and Schnaiberg, A. (2008) *The Treadmill of Production: injustice and unsustainability in the global economy*, Boulder (Colorado): Paradigm.

Grandclément, C. and Gaglio, G. (2011) 'Convoking the consumer in person: the focus group effect', in D. Zwick and J. Cayla (eds), *Inside Marketing: practices, ideologies, devices*, Oxford: Oxford University Press.

Granovetter, M. (1985) 'Economic action and social structure: the problem of embeddedness', *American Journal of Sociology*, 91(3): 481–510.

Greener, I. (2006) 'Nick Leeson and the collapse of Barings Bank: sociotechnical networks and the "rogue trader"', *Organization*, 3(3): 421–41.

Grossman, E., Luque, E. and Muniesa, F. (2008) 'Economies through transparency', in C. Garsten and M. Lindh de Montoya (eds), *Transparency in a New Global Order: unveiling organizational visions*, Cheltenham: Edward Elgar Publishing.

Guala, F. (2001) 'Building economic machines: the FCC auctions', *Studies in History and Philosophy of Science*, 32(3): 453–77.

——(2005) *The Methodology of Experimental Economics*, Cambridge: Cambridge University Press.

Guattari, F. (2011) *Lignes de Fuite: pour un autre monde de possibles*, La Tour d'Aigues: Éditions de l'Aube.

Guattari, F. and Alliez, É. (1983) 'Le capital en fin de compte: systèmes, structures et processus capitalistiques', *Change International*, 1: 100–6.

——(1984) 'Capitalistic systems, structures and processes', in F. Guattari, *Molecular Revolution: psychiatry and politics*, London: Penguin.

Guyer, J.I. (2004) *Marginal Gains: monetary transactions in Atlantic Africa*, Chicago: The University of Chicago Press.

——(2009) 'Composites, fictions, and risk: toward an ethnography of price', in C. Hann and K. Hart (eds), *Market and Society: the great transformation today*, Cambridge: Cambridge University Press.

——(2010) 'The eruption of tradition? On ordinality and calculation', *Anthropological Theory*, 10(1–2): 123–31.

Haack, S. (1996) '"We pragmatists..."; Peirce and Rorty in conversation', *Ágora: Papeles de Filosofía*, 15(1): 53–68.

Habermas, J. (2012) *La Constitution de l'Europe*, Paris: Gallimard.

Hacking, I. (1983) *Representing and Intervening: introductory topics in the philosophy of natural science*, Cambridge: Cambridge University Press.

——(2002a) 'Inaugural lecture: chair of philosophy and history of scientific concepts at the Collège de France, 16 January 2001', *Economy and Society*, 31(1): 1–14.

——(2002b) *Historical Ontology*, Cambridge (Massachusetts): Harvard University Press.

Hahn, C. and Hart, K. (eds) (2009) *Market and Society: The Great Transformation today*, Cambridge: Cambridge University Press.

Harman, G. (2009) *Prince of Networks: Bruno Latour and metaphysics*, Melbourne: Re.press.

Hatherly, D., Leung, D. and MacKenzie, D. (2008) 'The finitist accountant', in T. Pinch and R. Swedberg (eds), *Living in a Material World: economic*

sociology meets science and technology studies, Cambridge (Massachusetts): The MIT Press.
Hayek, F.A. (1945) 'The use of knowledge in society', *American Economic Review*, 35(4): 519–30.
Hecht, G. (1998) *The Radiance of France: nuclear power and national identity after World War II*, Cambridge (Massachusetts): The MIT Press.
Heidegger, M. (1958) *Essais et Conférences*, Paris: Gallimard.
Hennion, A. (2010) 'La question de la tonalité: retour sur le partage nature-culture. Relire Lévi-Strauss avec des lunettes pragmatistes?' *L'Année Sociologique*, 60: 361–86.
Hertz, E. (1998) *The Trading Crowd: an ethnography of the Shanghai stock market*, Cambridge: Cambridge University Press.
——(2000) 'Stock markets as "simulacra": observation that participates', *Tsantsa*, 5: 40–50.
Hetherington, K. (2007) *Capitalism's Eye: cultural spaces of the commodity*, London, Routledge.
Holm, P. and Nolde Nielsen, K. (2007) 'Framing fish, making markets: the construction of individual transferable quotas (ITQs)', in M. Callon, Y. Millo and F. Muniesa (eds), *Market Devices*, Oxford: Blackwell.
Hood, C. (2000) *The Art of the State: culture, rhetoric and public management*, Oxford: Oxford University Press.
——(2006) 'Gaming in targetworld: the targets approach to managing British public services', *Public Administration Review*, 66(4): 515–21.
——(2007) 'Public service management by numbers: why does it vary? Where has it come from? What are the gaps and the puzzles?' *Public Money and Management*, 27(2): 95–102.
Hopwood, A.G. and Miller, P. (eds) (1994) *Accounting as Social and Institutional Practice*, Cambridge: Cambridge University Press.
Huault, I. and Rainelli-Le Montagner, H. (2009) 'Market shaping as an answer to ambiguities: the case of credit derivatives', *Organization Studies*, 30(5): 549–75.
Ibáñez, J. (1985) *Del Algoritmo al Sujeto: perspectivas de la investigación social*, Madrid: Siglo XXI.
——(ed.) (1990) *Nuevos Avances en la Investigación Social: la investigación social de segundo orden*, Barcelona: Anthropos.
——(1991) *El Regreso del Sujeto: la investigación social de segundo orden*, Santiago de Chile: Amerinda.
Ingrao, B. and Israel, G. (1987) *La Mano Invisibile: l'equilibrio economico nella storia della scienza*, Rome: Laterza.
——(1990) *The Invisible Hand: economic equilibrium in the history of science*, Cambridge (Massachusetts): The MIT Press.
Izquierdo, A.J. (2001) 'Reliability at risk: the supervision of financial models as a case study for reflexive economic sociology', *European Societies*, 3(1): 69–90.

—— (2004) 'Procedimientos de restauración del sentido ordinario de la realidad: un estudio de las secuencias de revelación de las bromas de cámara oculta', *Revista Española de Investigaciones Sociológicas*, 106: 103–38.

Izquierdo Martín, A.J. (1996) 'Equilibrio económico y racionalidad maquínica: del algoritmo al sujeto en el análisis económico moderno', *Política y Sociedad*, 21: 89–111.

James, W. (1907) 'What pragmatism means', *Popular Science Monthly*, 70 (April): 351–64.

—— (2000) *Pragmatism and Other Writings*, London: Penguin Books.

Jany-Catrice, F. (2012) *La Performance Totale: nouvel esprit du capitalisme?* Villeneuve-d'Ascq: Septentrion.

Jensen, C.B. (2004) 'A nonhumanist disposition: on performativity, practical ontology, and intervention', *Configurations*, 12(2): 229–61.

Joyce, P. (2013) *The State of Freedom: a social history of the British state since 1800*, Cambridge: Cambridge University Press.

Kaplan, S. (2011) 'Strategy and PowerPoint: an inquiry into the epistemic culture and machinery of strategy making', *Organization Science*, 22(2): 320–46.

Karl, A.G. (2013) '"Bank talk", performativity and financial markets', *Journal of Cultural Economy*, 6(1): 61–77.

Karpik, L. (2007) *L'Économie des Singularités*, Paris: Gallimard.

—— (2010) *Valuing the Unique: the economics of singularities*, Princeton (New Jersey): Princeton University Press.

Keating, P. and Cambrosio, A. (2003) *Biomedical Platforms: realigning the normal and the pathological in late-twentieth-century medicine*, Cambridge (Massachusetts): The MIT Press.

Khurana, R. (2007) *From Higher Aims to Hired Hands: the social transformation of American business schools and the unfulfilled promise of management as a profession*, Princeton (New Jersey): Princeton University Press.

Khurana, R. and Snook, S.A. (2004) 'Developing leaders of character: lessons from West Point', in R. Gandossy and J. Sonnenfeld (eds), *Leadership and Governance from the Inside Out*, Hoboken (New Jersey): Wiley.

Kjellberg, H. and Helgesson, C.-F. (2006) 'Multiple versions of markets: multiplicity and performativity in market practice', *Industrial Marketing Management*, 35(7): 839–55.

—— (2007) 'On the nature of markets and their practices', *Marketing Theory*, 7(2): 137–62.

Klossowski, P. (1963) 'À propos du simulacre dans la communication de Georges Bataille', *Critique*, 19(195–6): 742–50.

Klossowski, P. and Zucca, P. (1970) *La Monnaie Vivante*, Paris: Eric Losfeld.

Knights, D. and Willmott, H. (1999) *Management Lives: power and identity in work organizations*, Thousand Oaks: Sage.

Knoblauch, H. (2008) 'The performance of knowledge: pointing and knowledge in PowerPoint presentations', *Cultural Sociology*, 2(1): 75–97.
Knorr Cetina, K. and Bruegger, U. (2002) 'Global microstructures: the virtual societies of financial markets', *American Journal of Sociology*, 107(4): 905–50.
Knuth, D.E. (1977) 'Algorithms', *Scientific American*, 236(4): 63–80.
Kochan, J. (2010) 'Latour's Heidegger', *Social Studies of Science*, 40(4): 579–98.
Kockelman, P. (2013) *Agent, Person, Subject, Self: a theory of ontology, interaction, and infrastructure*, Oxford: Oxford University Press.
Koppel, M., Atlan, H. and Dupuy, J.-P. (1987) 'Von Foerster's conjecture: trivial machines and alienation in systems', *International Journal of General Systems*, 13(3): 257–64.
Korn, J.H. (1997) *Illusions of Reality: a history of deception in social psychology*, Albany: State University of New York Press.
Kosofsky Sedgwick, E. (2003) *Touching Feeling: affect, pedagogy, performativity*, Durham (North Carolina): Duke University Press.
Krawiec, K.D. (2009) 'The return of the rogue', *Arizona Law Review*, 51(1): 127–74.
Kregel, J.A. (1995) 'Neoclassical price theory, institutions, and the evolution of securities market organisation', *The Economic Journal*, 105(429): 459–70.
Krippner, G.R. (2011) *Capitalizing on Crisis: the political origins of the rise of finance*, Cambridge (Massachusetts): Harvard University Press.
Kusch, M. (2010) 'Hacking's historical epistemology: a critique of styles of reasoning', *Studies in History and Philosophy of Science Part A*, 41(2): 158–73.
Lamo de Espinosa, E. (1990) *La Sociedad Reflexiva: sujeto y objeto del conocimiento sociológico*, Madrid: Siglo XXI.
Langley, P. (2008) *The Everyday Life of Global Finance: saving and borrowing in Anglo-America*, Oxford: Oxford University Press.
Lascoumes, P. and Le Galès, P. (2007) 'Understanding public policy through its instruments: from the nature of instruments to the sociology of public policy instrumentation', *Governance*, 20(1): 1–21.
Lash, S. and Lury, C. (2007) *Global Culture Industry: the mediation of things*, Cambridge: Polity Press.
Latour, B. (1987) *Science in Action: how to follow scientists and engineers through society*, Milton Keynes: Open University Press.
——(1990) 'The force and the reason of experiment', in H.E. Le Grand (ed.), *Experimental Inquiries: historical, philosophical and social studies of experimentation in science*, Dordrecht: Kluwer.
——(1991) *Nous N'Avons Jamais Été Modernes: essai d'anthropologie symétrique*, Paris: La Découverte.
——(1993a) *We Have Never Been Modern*, Cambridge (Massachusetts): Harvard University Press.

——(1993b) 'Pasteur on lactic acid yeast: a partial semiotic analysis', *Configurations*, 1(1): 129–46.
——(1996) 'Foreword: the flat-earthers of social theory', in M. Power (ed.), *Accounting and Science: natural inquiry and commercial reason*, Cambridge: Cambridge University Press.
——(1999) *Pandora's Hope: essays on the reality of science studies*, Cambridge (Massachusetts): Harvard University Press.
——(2000) 'On the partial existence of existing and nonexisting objects', in L. Daston (ed.), *Biographies of Scientific Objects*, Chicago: The University of Chicago Press.
——(2006) 'Air', in C.A. Jones (ed.), *Sensorium: embodied experience, technology, and contemporary art*, Cambridge (Massachusetts): The MIT Press.
——(2009) 'Will non-humans be saved? An argument in ecotheology', *Journal of the Royal Anthropological Institute*, 15(3): 459–75.
——(2010a) 'Coming out as a philosopher', *Social Studies of Science*, 4(4): 599–608.
——(2010b) 'A plea for earthly sciences', in J. Burnett, S. Jeffers and G. Thomas (eds), *New Social Connections: sociology's subjects and objects*, Basingstoke: Palgrave Macmillan.
——(2012) *Enquête sur les Modes d'Existence: une anthropologie des modernes*, Paris: La Découverte.
Latour, B., Harman, G. and Erdélyi, P. (2011) *The Prince and the Wolf: Latour and Harman at the LSE*, Alresford: Zero Books.
Laval, C. (2007), *L'Homme Économique: essai sur les racines du néolibéralisme*, Paris: Gallimard.
Law, J. (1994) *Organizing Modernity*, Oxford: Blackwell.
——(2002) 'Economics as interference', in P. du Gay and M. Pryke (eds), *Cultural Economy: cultural analysis and commercial life*, London: Sage.
——(2004) *After Method: mess in social science research*, London: Routledge.
Lears, J. (2009) *Rebirth of a Nation: the making of modern America, 1877–1920*, New York: HarperCollins.
Lee, R. (1998) *What is an Exchange? The automation, management, and regulation of financial markets*, Oxford: Oxford University Press.
Legendre, P. (1988) *Le Désir Politique de Dieu: étude sur les montages de l'État et du droit*, Paris: Fayard.
——(1992) *Trésor Historique de l'État en France: l'administration classique*, Paris: Fayard.
Lenglet, M. (2011) 'Conflicting codes and codings: how algorithmic trading is reshaping financial regulation', *Theory, Culture & Society*, 28(6): 44–66.
Lépinay, V.-A. (2007a) 'Decoding finance: articulation and liquidity around a trading room', in D. MacKenzie, F. Muniesa and L. Siu (eds), *Do Economists Make Markets? On the performativity of economics*, Princeton (New Jersey): Princeton University Press.

——(2007b) 'Parasitic formulae: the case of capital guarantee products', in M. Callon, Y. Millo and F. Muniesa (eds), *Market Devices*, Oxford: Blackwell.

——(2011) *Codes of Finance: engineering derivatives in a global bank*, Princeton (New Jersey): Princeton University Press.

Lépinay, V.-A. and Callon, M. (2009) 'Sketch of derivations in Wall Street and Atlantic Africa', in C.S. Chapman, D.J. Cooper and P. Miller (eds), *Accounting, Organizations, and Institutions: essays in honour of Anthony Hopwood*, Oxford: Oxford University Press.

Lepori, B., Barré, R. and Filliatreau, G. (2008) 'New perspectives and challenges for the design and production of S&T indicators', *Research Evaluation*, 17(1): 33–44.

Lévi-Strauss, C. (1949) 'L'efficacité symbolique', *Revue de l'Histoire des Religions*, 135(1): 5–27.

Leyshon, A. and Thrift, N. (1997) *Money/Space: geographies of monetary transformation*, London: Routledge.

Lezaun, J. (2007a) 'A market of opinions: the political epistemology of focus groups', in M. Callon, Y. Millo and F. Muniesa (eds), *Market Devices*, Oxford: Blackwell.

——(2007b) 'Experiment', in G. Ritzer (ed.), *Blackwell Encyclopedia of Sociology*, Oxford: Blackwell.

Lezaun, J., Muniesa, F. and Vikkelsø, S. (2013) 'Provocative containment and the drift of social-scientific realism', *Journal of Cultural Economy*, 6(3): 278–93.

Linhardt, D. (2012) 'Épreuves d'État: une variation sur la définition wébérienne de l'État', *Quaderni*, 78: 1–19.

Linhardt, D. and Moreau de Bellaing, C. (2005) 'Légitime violence? Enquête sur la réalité de l'État démocratique', *Revue Française de Science Politique*, 55(2): 269–98.

Linhardt, D. and Muniesa, F. (2011a) 'Du ministère à l'agence: étude d'un processus d'altération politique', *Politix*, 95: 73–102.

——(2011b) 'Tenir lieu de politique: le paradoxe des politiques d'économisation', *Politix*, 95: 9–21.

Lohmann, L. (2009) 'Toward a different debate in environmental accounting: the cases of carbon and cost-benefit', *Accounting, Organizations and Society*, 34(3–4): 499–534.

Lordon, F. (1997) *Les Quadratures de la Politique Économique: les infortunes de la vertu*, Paris: Albin Michel.

——(2002) *Politique du Capital*, Paris: Odile Jacob.

Lorino, P. (1989) *L'Économiste et le Manageur: éléments de micro-économie pour une nouvelle gestion*, Paris: La Découverte.

Lorino, P. and Teulier, R. (eds) (2005) *Entre Connaissance et Organisation: l'activité collective*, Paris: La Découverte.

Lounsbury, M. and Crumley, E.T. (2007) 'New practice creation: an institutional perspective on innovation', *Organization Studies*, 28(7): 993–1012.

Loxley, J. (2007) *Performativity*, London: Routledge.
Luhmann, N. (1993) *Risk: a sociological theory*, Berlin: Walter de Gruyter.
Lyotard, J.-F. (1979a) *Les Problèmes du Savoir dans les Sociétés Industrielles les Plus Développées*, Paris and Québec: Université de Paris VIII (Vincennes) and Conseil des Universités du Gouvernement de Québec.
——(1979b) *La Condition Postmoderne: rapport sur le savoir*, Paris: Éditions de Minuit.
——(1984) *The Postmodern Condition: a report on knowledge*, Minneapolis (Minnesota): University of Minnesota Press.
McCarthy, A. (2004) '"Stanley Milgram, Allen Funt, and me": postwar social science and the "first wave" of reality TV', in S. Murray and L. Ouellette (eds), *Reality TV: remaking television culture*, New York: New York University Press.
McFall, L. (2004) *Advertising: a cultural economy*, London: Sage.
MacKenzie, D. (1989) 'From Kwajalein to Armageddon? Testing and the social construction of missile accuracy', in D. Gooding, T. Pinch and S. Schaffer (eds), *The Use of Experiment: studies in the natural sciences*, Cambridge: Cambridge University Press.
——(2001) 'Physics and finance: S-terms and modern finance as a topic for science studies', *Science, Technology & Human Values*, 26(2): 115–44.
——(2003) 'An equation and its worlds: bricolage, exemplars, disunity and performativity in financial economics', *Social Studies of Science*, 33(6): 831–68.
——(2004) 'The big, bad wolf and the rational market: portfolio insurance, the 1987 crash and the performativity of economics', *Economy and Society*, 33(3): 303–34.
——(2006) *An Engine, Not a Camera: how financial models shape markets*, Cambridge (Massachusetts): The MIT Press.
——(2007) 'Is economics performative? Option theory and the construction of derivative markets', in D. MacKenzie, F. Muniesa and L. Siu (eds), *Do Economists Make Markets? On the performativity of economics*, Princeton (New Jersey): Princeton University Press.
——(2009) 'Making things the same: gases, emission rights and the politics of carbon markets', *Accounting, Organizations and Society*, 34(3–4): 440–55.
MacKenzie, D. and Millo, Y. (2003) 'Constructing a market, performing theory: the historical sociology of a financial derivatives exchange', *American Journal of Sociology*, 109(1): 107–45.
MacKenzie, D., Muniesa, F. and Siu, L. (eds) (2007) *Do Economists Make Markets? On the performativity of economics*, Princeton (New Jersey): Princeton University Press.
MacKenzie, D., Beunza, D., Millo, Y. and Pardo-Guerra, J.-P. (2012) 'Drilling through the Allegheny Mountains: liquidity, materiality and high-frequency trading', *Journal of Cultural Economy*, 5(3): 279–96.

McNair, M.P. (ed.) (1954) *The Case Method at the Harvard Business School: papers by present and past members of the faculty and staff*, New York: McGraw-Hill.

Majury, N. (2007) 'Technology and the architecture of markets: reconfiguring the Canadian equity market', *Environment and Planning A*, 39(9): 2187–206.

Mangham, I.L. (1990) 'Managing as a performing art', *British Journal of Management*, 1(2): 105–15.

Mattei, U. and Nader, L. (2008) *Plunder: when the rule of law is illegal*, Oxford: Blackwell.

Maurer, B. (2002a) 'Anthropological and accounting knowledge in Islamic banking and finance: rethinking critical accounts', *Journal of the Royal Anthropological Institute*, 8(4): 645–67.

——(2002b) 'Repressed futures: financial derivatives' theological unconscious', *Economy and Society*, 31(1): 15–36.

——(2005) *Mutual Life, Limited: Islamic banking, alternative currencies, lateral reason*, Princeton (New Jersey): Princeton University Press.

——(2006) 'The anthropology of money', *Annual Review of Anthropology*, 35: 15–36.

——(2007) 'Incalculable payments: money, scale, and the South African offshore grey money amnesty', *African Studies Review*, 50(2): 125–38.

Menand, L. (2001) *The Metaphysical Club: a story of ideas in America*, New York: Farrar, Straus and Giroux.

Merton, R.K. (1987) 'The focussed interview and focus groups: continuities and discontinuities', *Public Opinion Quarterly*, 51(4): 550–66.

Merton, R.K. and Kendall, P.L. (1946) 'The focused interview', *American Journal of Sociology*, 51(6): 541–57.

Miller, P. (1994) 'Accounting and objectivity: the invention of calculating selves and calculable spaces' in A. Megill (ed.), *Rethinking Objectivity*, Durham (North Carolina): Duke University Press.

Miller, P. and Rose, N. (2008) *Governing the Present: administering economic, social and personal life*, Cambridge: Polity Press.

Millo, Y. (2007) 'Making things deliverable: the origins of index-based derivatives', in M. Callon, Y. Millo and F. Muniesa (eds), *Market Devices*, Oxford: Blackwell.

Millo, Y. and MacKenzie, D. (2009) 'The usefulness of inaccurate models: towards an understanding of the emergence of financial risk management', *Accounting, Organizations and Society*, 34(5): 638–53.

Millo, Y., Muniesa, F., Panourgias, N.S. and Scott, S.V. (2005) 'Organised detachment: clearinghouse mechanisms in financial markets', *Information and Organization*, 15(3): 229–46.

Mirowski, P. (1989) *More Heat than Light: economics as social physics, physics as nature's economics*, Cambridge: Cambridge University Press.

——(1996) '¿Sueñan las máquinas? De los agentes económicos como cyborgs', *Política y Sociedad*, 21: 113–31.

——(2002) *Machine Dreams: economics becomes a cyborg science*, Cambridge: Cambridge University Press.

——(2007) 'Markets come to bits: evolution, computation and markomata in economic science', *Journal of Economic Behavior and Organization*, 63(2): 209–42.

Mirowski, P. and Nik-Khah, E. (2007) 'Markets made flesh: performativity, and a problem in science studies, augmented with consideration of the FCC auctions', in D. MacKenzie, F. Muniesa and L. Siu (eds), *Do Economists Make Markets? On the performativity of economics*, Princeton (New Jersey): Princeton University Press.

Mirowski, P. and Plehwe, D. (eds) (2009) *The Road from Mont Pèlerin: the making of the neoliberal thought collective*, Cambridge (Massachusetts): Harvard University Press.

Mirowski, P. and Somefun, K. (1998) 'Markets as evolving computational entities', *Journal of Evolutionary Economics*, 8(4): 329–56.

Mitchell, T. (1991) *Colonising Egypt*, Berkeley (California): University of California Press.

——(1998) 'Fixing the economy', *Cultural Studies*, 12(1): 82–101.

——(2002) *Rule of Experts: Egypt, techno-politics, modernity*, Berkeley (California): University of California Press.

——(2005) 'The work of economics: how a discipline makes its world', *European Journal of Sociology*, 46(2): 297–320.

——(2007) 'The properties of markets', in D. MacKenzie, F. Muniesa and L. Siu (eds), *Do Economists Make Markets? On the performativity of economics*, Princeton (New Jersey): Princeton University Press.

——(2008) 'Rethinking economy', *Geoforum*, 39(3): 1116–21.

——(2009) 'Carbon democracy', *Economy and Society*, 38(3): 399–432.

——(2010) 'The resources of economics: making the 1973 oil crisis', *Journal of Cultural Economy*, 3(2): 181–204.

Modell, S. (2001) 'Performance measurement and institutional processes: a study of managerial responses to public sector reform', *Management Accounting Research*, 12(4): 437–64.

——(2009) 'Institutional research on performance measurement and management in the public sector accounting literature: a review and assessment', *Financial Accounting and Management*, 25(3): 277–303.

Modigliani, F. and Miller, M.H. (1958) 'The cost of capital, corporation finance and the theory of investment', *The American Economic Review*, 48(3): 261–97.

Moisdon, J.-C. (ed.) (1997) *Du Mode d'Existence des Outils de Gestion: les instruments de gestion à l'épreuve de l'organisation*, Paris: Seli Arslan.

Mol, A. (2002) *The Body Multiple: ontology in medical practice*, Durham (North Carolina): Duke University Press.

Moodie, J. (2009) 'Internal systems and controls that help to prevent rogue trading', *Journal of Securities Operations & Custody*, 2(2): 169–80.

Morgan, M.S. and Den Butter, F. (eds) (2000) *Empirical Models and Policy Making: interaction and institutions*, London: Routledge.

Muniesa, F. (2000a) 'Performing prices: the case of price discovery automation in the financial markets', in H. Kalthoff, R. Rottenburg and H.-J. Wagener (eds), *Facts and Figures: economic representations and practices*, Marburg: Metropolis-Verlag.

——(2000b) 'Un robot walrasien: cotation électronique et justesse de la découverte des prix', *Politix*, 52: 121–54.

——(2005) 'Contenir le marché: la transition de la criée à la cotation électronique à la Bourse de Paris', *Sociologie du Travail*, 47(4): 485–501.

——(2007) 'Market technologies and the pragmatics of prices', *Economy and Society*, 36(3): 377–95.

——(2008a) 'Attachment and detachment in the economy' in P. Redman (ed.), *Attachment: sociology and social worlds*, Manchester: Manchester University Press.

——(2008b) 'Trading-room telephones and the identification of counterparts', in T. Pinch and R. Swedberg (eds), *Living in a Material World: economic sociology meets science and technology studies*, Cambridge (Massachusetts): The MIT Press.

——(2010) 'Cooling down and heating up: a stress test on politics and economics', in M. Akrich, Y. Barthe, F. Muniesa and P. Mustar (eds), *Débordements: mélanges offerts à Michel Callon*, Paris: Presses des Mines.

——(2011a) 'Is a stock exchange a computer solution? Explicitness, algorithms and the Arizona Stock Exchange', *International Journal of Actor-Network Theory and Technological Innovation*, 3(1): 1–15.

——(2011b) 'Javier Izquierdo and the methodology of reality', *Journal of Cultural Economy*, 4(1): 109–11.

——(2012) 'A flank movement in the understanding of valuation', in L. Adkins and C. Lury (eds), *Measure and Value*, Oxford: Wiley-Blackwell.

——(2013) 'Politiser, économiser la commande', in D. Debaise, X. Douroux, C. Joschke, A. Pontégnie and K. Solhdju (eds), *Faire Art Comme On Fait Société: les Nouveaux commanditaires*, Dijon: Presses du Réel.

Muniesa, F. and Callon, M. (2007) 'Economic experiments and the construction of markets', in D. MacKenzie, F. Muniesa and L. Siu (eds), *Do Economists Make Markets? On the performativity of economics*, Princeton (New Jersey): Princeton University Press.

——(2009) 'La performativité des sciences économiques', in P. Steiner and F. Vatin (eds), *Traité de Sociologie Économique*, Paris: PUF.

Muniesa, F. and Linhardt, D. (2011) 'Trials of explicitness in the implementation of public management reform', *Critical Perspectives on Accounting*, 22(6): 550–66.

Muniesa, F. and Trébuchet-Breitwiller, A.-S. (2010) 'Becoming a measuring instrument: an ethnography of perfume consumer testing', *Journal of Cultural Economy*, 3(3): 321–37.

Muniesa, F., Millo, Y. and Callon, M. (2007) 'An introduction to market devices', in M. Callon, Y. Millo and F. Muniesa (eds), *Market Devices*, Oxford: Blackwell.

Muniesa, F., Chabert, D., Ducrocq-Grondin, M. and Scott, S.V. (2011) 'Back-office intricacy: the description of financial objects in an investment bank', *Industrial and Corporate Change*, 20(4): 1189–213.

Nader, L. (2002) *The Life of the Law: anthropological projects*, Berkeley (California): University of California Press.

Naville, P. (1963) *Vers l'Automatisme Social? Problème du travail et de l'automation*, Paris: Gallimard.

Nitzan, J. and Bichler, S. (2009) *Capital as Power: a study of order and creorder*, London: Routledge.

Noël, D. (2007) 'Le virtuel selon Deleuze', *Intellectica*, 45(1): 109–27.

Noussair, C., Robin, S. and Ruffieux, B. (2002) 'Do consumers not care about biotech foods or do they just not read the labels?', *Economics Letters*, 75(1): 47–53.

——(2003) 'De l'opinion publique aux comportements des consommateurs: faut-il une filière Sans OGM?', *Revue Économique*, 54(1): 47–70.

——(2004a) 'Do consumers really refuse to buy genetically modified food?', *The Economic Journal*, 114(492): 102–20.

——(2004b) 'A comparison of hedonic rating and demand-revealing auctions', *Food Quality and Preference*, 15(4): 393–402.

——(2004c) 'Revealing consumers' willingness-to-pay: a comparison of the BDM mechanism and the Vickrey auction', *Journal of Economic Psychology*, 25(6): 725–41.

Ogien, A. (1995) *L'Esprit Gestionnaire: une analyse de l'air du temps*, Paris: Éditions de l'EHESS.

——(2007) 'La gouvernance, ou le mépris du politique', *Cités*, 32: 137–56.

——(2010) 'La valeur sociale du chiffre: la quantification de l'action publique entre performance et démocratie', *Revue Française de Socio-Économie*, 5: 19–40.

Ortiz, H. (2011) 'Marchés efficients, investisseurs libres et États garants: trames du politique dans les pratiques financières professionnelles', *Politix*, 95: 155–80.

——(2012) '"Dans ses tendances, l'industrie financière ne se trompe pas, mais elle exagère toujours": enjeux moraux dans les pratiques professionnelles de la finance', in D. Fassin and J.-S. Eideliman (eds), *Économies Morales Contemporaines*, Paris: La Découverte.

——(2013a) 'Financial professionals as a global elite', in J. Abbink and T. Salverda (eds), *The Anthropology of Elites: power, culture and the complexities of distinction*, Basingstoke: Palgrave Macmillan.

——(2013b) 'La "valeur" dans l'industrie financière: le prix des actions cotées comme "vérité" technique et politique', *L'Année Sociologique*, 63: 107–36.

——(2013c) 'Financial value: economic, moral, political, global', *HAU: Journal of Ethnographic Theory*, 3(1): 64–79.

Osborne, D. and Hutchinson, P. (2004) *The Price of Government: getting the results we need in an age of permanent fiscal crisis*, New York: Basic Books.
Peirce, C.S. (1905) 'What pragmatism is', *The Monist*, 15(2): 161–81.
Perkmann, M. and Spicer, A. (2010) 'What are business models? Developing a theory of performative representations', in N. Phillips, D. Griffiths and G. Sewell (eds), *Technology and Organization Essays in Honour of Joan Woodward*, Bingley: Emerald.
Pickering, A. (1995) *The Mangle of Practice: time, agency and science*, Chicago: The University of Chicago Press.
Pinch, T. (1993) '"Testing – one, two, three… testing!": towards a sociology of testing', *Science, Technology & Human Values*, 18(1): 25–41.
Pipan, T. and Czarniawska, B. (2010) 'How to construct an actor-network: management accounting from idea to practice', *Critical Perspectives on Accounting*, 21(3): 243–51.
Poister, T.H. (2003) *Measuring Performance in Public and Nonprofit Organizations*, San Francisco: Jossey-Bass.
Polanyi, K. (1944) *The Great Transformation: the political and economic origins of our time*, New York: Rinehart & Company.
Pontille, D. (2004) *La Signature Scientifique: une sociologie pragmatique de l'attribution*, Paris: CNRS Éditions.
Pontille, D. and Torny, D. (2013) 'La manufacture de l'évaluation scientifique: algorithmes, jeux de données et outils bibliométriques', *Réseaux*, 177: 23–61.
Powell, W.W. and DiMaggio, P.J. (eds) (1991) *The New Institutionalism in Organizational Analysis*, Chicago: The University of Chicago Press.
Power, M. (ed.) (1996) *Accounting and Science: natural inquiry and commercial reason*, Cambridge: Cambridge University Press.
——(2005) 'The invention of operational risk', *Review of International Political Economy*, 12(4): 577–99.
——(2007) *Organized Uncertainty: designing a world of risk management*, Oxford: Oxford University Press.
Preda, A. (2001) 'In the enchanted grove: financial conversations and the marketplace in England and France in the 18th century', *Journal of Historical Sociology*, 14(3): 276–307.
——(2003) 'Les hommes de la Bourse et leurs instruments merveilleux: technologies de transmission des cours et origines de l'organisation des marchés modernes', *Réseaux*, 122: 137–64.
——(2006) 'Socio-technical agency in financial markets: the case of the stock ticker', *Social Studies of Science*, 36(5): 753–82.
——(2009) *Framing Finance: the boundaries of markets and modern capitalism*, Chicago: The University of Chicago Press.
Previtali, R. (2009) 'Operational risk control: Société Générale and other well-known cases', *Journal of Securities Operations & Custody*, 2(1): 24–36.

Purcell, E.A. Jr (1973) *The Crisis of Democratic Theory: scientific naturalism and the problem of value*, Lexington (Kentucky): The University Press of Kentucky.

Quattrone, P. (2009) 'Books to be practiced: memory, the power of the visual, and the success of accounting', *Accounting, Organizations and Society*, 34(1): 85–118.

Récanati, F. (1982) *Les Énoncés Performatifs: contribution à la pragmatique*, Paris: Éditions de Minuit.

Rawls, A.W. (2008), 'Harold Garfinkel, ethnomethodology and workplace studies', *Organization Studies*, 29(5): 701–32.

Ripley, W.Z. (1915) *Railroads: finance and organization*, New York: Longmans, Green & Co.

Robé, J.-P. (1999) *L'Entreprise et le Droit*, Paris: PUF.

——(2011) 'The legal structure of the firm', *Accounting, Economics and Law*, 1(1): 1–86.

Robson, K. (1991) 'On the arenas of accounting change: the process of translation', *Accounting, Organizations and Society*, 16(5–6): 547–70.

——(1992) 'Accounting numbers as "inscription": action at a distance and the development of accounting', *Accounting, Organizations and Society*, 17(7): 685–708.

——(1993) 'Governing science and economic growth at a distance: accounting representation and the management of research and development', *Economy and Society*, 22(4): 461–81.

——(1994) 'Connecting science to the economic: accounting calculation and the visibility of research and development', *Science in Context*, 7(3): 497–514.

Roitman, J.L. (2007) 'The efficacy of the economy', *African Studies Review*, 50(2): 155–61.

Ronell, A. (2005) *The Test Drive*, Champaign (Illinois): University of Illinois Press.

Rouby, C., Schaal, B., Dubois, D., Gervais, R. and Holley, A. (eds) (2002) *Olfaction, Taste and Cognition*, Cambridge: Cambridge University Press.

Rowe, C. and Slutzky, R. (1963) 'Transparency: literal and phenomenal', *Perspecta*, 8, 45–54.

Roy, W.G. (1997) *Socializing Capital: the rise of the large industrial corporation in America*, Princeton (New Jersey): Princeton University Press.

Sahlins, M. (2008) *The Western Illusion of Human Nature: with reflections on the long history of hierarchy, equality and the sublimation of anarchy in the West, and comparative notes on other conceptions of the human condition*, Chicago: Prickly Paradigm Press.

Schinckus, C. (2008) 'The financial simulacrum: the consequences of the symbolization and the computerization of the financial market', *Journal of Socio-Economics*, 37(3): 1076–89.

Schmitt, C. (2007) *The Concept of the Political*, expanded edn, Chicago: The University of Chicago Press.
Schwartz, R.A. (ed.) (2001) *The Electronic Call Auction: market mechanism and trading*, Boston: Kluwer Academic Publishers.
Schwartz, R.A., Byrne, J.A. and Colaninno, A. (eds) (2003) *Call Auction Trading: new answers to old questions*, Boston: Kluwer Academic Publishers.
Sechehaye, M.-A. (1947) *La Réalisation Symbolique: nouvelle methode de psychothérapie appliquée à un cas de schizophrénie*, Bern: Hans Huber.
Segrestin, D. (2004) *Les Chantiers du Manager*, Paris: Armand Colin.
Serres, M. (1974) *Hermès III: la traduction*, Paris: Éditions de Minuit.
Shell, M. (1982) *Money, Language, and Thought: literary and philosophic economies from the medieval to the modern era*, Berkeley (California): University of California Press.
Sims, B. (1999) 'Concrete practices: testing in an earthquake-engineering laboratory', *Social Studies of Science,* 29(4): 483–518.
Sloterdijk, P. (2009a) *Terror from the Air*, Los Angeles: Semiotext(e).
——(2009b) 'Airquakes', *Environment and Planning D: Society and Space*, 27(1): 41–57.
Smith, D.W. (2005) 'The concept of the simulacrum: Deleuze and the overturning of platonism', *Continental Philosophy Review*, 38(1–2): 89–123.
Smith, V.L. (1994), 'Economics in the laboratory', *Journal of Economic Perspectives*, 8(1): 113–31.
Snook, S.A., Nohria, N.N. and Khurana, R. (eds) (2012) *The Handbook for Teaching Leadership: knowing, doing, and being*, Thousand Oaks: Sage.
Sombart, N. (1999) *Les Mâles Vertus des Allemands: autour du syndrome Carl Schmitt*, Paris: Cerf.
Spicer, A., Alvesson, M. and Kärreman, D. (2009) 'Critical performativity: the unfinished business of critical management studies', *Human Relations*, 62(4): 537–60.
Stark, D. (2009) *The Sense of Dissonance: accounts of worth in economic life*, Princeton (New Jersey): Princeton University Press.
Stark, D. and Paravel, V. (2008) 'PowerPoint in public: digital technologies and the new morphology of demonstration', *Theory, Culture & Society*, 25(5): 30–55.
Swiercz, P.M. and Ross, K.T. (2003) 'Rational, human, political, and symbolic text in Harvard Business School cases: a study of structure and content', *Journal of Management Education*, 27(4): 407–30.
Taylor, J.R. and Van Every, E.J. (2000) *The Emergent Organization: communication as its site and surface*, Mahwah (New Jersey): Lawrence Erlbaum Associates.
——(2010) *The Situated Organization: case studies in the pragmatics of communication research*, London: Routledge.

Bibliography

Teil, G. and Muniesa, F. (2006) 'Donner un prix: observations à partir d'un dispositif d'économie expérimentale', *Terrains & Travaux*, 11: 222–44.

Teira Serrano, D. (2001) 'Lo uno y lo múltiple: la estructura de la explicación económica en Walras y Marshall', in A. Ávila, W.J. González and G. Marqués (eds), *Ciencia Económica y Economía de la Ciencia*, Madrid: FCE.

Thévenot, L. (1984) 'Rules and implements: investments in forms', *Social Science Information*, 23(1): 1–45.

Thomas, Y. (2011) *Les Operations du Droit*, Paris: Seuil.

Thrift, N. (2005) *Knowing Capitalism*, London: Sage.

Towl, A.R. (1969) *To Study Administration by Cases*, Boston: Harvard University, Graduate School of Business Administration.

Townley, B., Cooper, D.J. and Oakes, L. (2003) 'Performance measures and the rationalization of organizations', *Organization Studies*, 24(7): 1045–71.

Trébuchet-Breitwiller, A.-S. and Muniesa, F. (2010). 'L'emprise des tests: comment les tests marketing agencent le marché de la parfumerie fine', in A. Hatchuel, O. Favereau and F. Aggeri (eds), *L'Activité Marchande sans le Marché?* Paris: Presses des Mines.

Valdés, J.G. (1995) *Pinochet's Economists: the Chicago School in Chile*, Cambridge: Cambridge University Press.

Vatin, F. (1987) *La Fluidité Industrielle: essai sur la théorie de la production et le devenir du travail*, Paris: Méridiens Klincskieck.

Verran, H. (2007) 'The telling challenge of Africa's economies', *African Studies Review*, 50(2): 163–82.

Viveiros de Castro, E. (1988) 'Cosmological deixis and Amerindian perspectivism', *Journal of the Royal Anthropological Institute*, 4(3): 469–88.

——(2004) 'Exchanging perspectives: the transformation of objects into subjects in Amerindian ontologies', *Common Knowledge*, 10(3): 463–84.

Von Foerster, H. (2003) *Understanding Understanding: essays on cybernetics and cognition*, New York: Springer-Verlag.

Walker, D.A. (2001) 'A factual account of the functioning of the nineteenth-century Paris Bourse', *European Journal of the History of Economic Thought*, 8(2): 186–207.

Walras, L. (1926) *Éléments d'Économie Politique Pure ou Théorie de la Richesse Sociale*, Paris: Pichon et Durand-Auzias.

Weick, K.E. (1995) *Sensemaking in Organizations*, Thousand Oaks: Sage.

Will, C. and Moreira, T. (eds) (2010) *Medical Proofs, Social Experiments: clinical trials in shifting contexts*, Farnham: Ashgate.

Yates, J. and Orlikowski, W. (2007) 'The PowerPoint presentation and its corollaries: how genres shape communicative action in organizations', in M. Zachry and C. Thralls (eds), *Communicative Practices in Workplaces and the Professions: cultural perspectives on the regulation of discourse and organizations*, Amityville (New York): Baywood Publishing.

Zelizer, V.A. (1985) *Pricing the Priceless Child: the changing social value of children*, New York: Basic Books.

——(1997) *The Social Meaning of Money: pin money, paychecks, poor relief, and other currencies*, Princeton (New Jersey): Princeton University Press.

——(2005) *The Purchase of Intimacy*, Princeton (New Jersey): Princeton University Press.

——(2010) *Economic Lives: how culture shapes the economy*, Princeton (New Jersey): Princeton University Press.

Zwick, D. and Cayla, J. (2011) *Inside Marketing: practices, ideologies, devices*, Oxford: Oxford University Press.

Index

accounting 29, 33, 55–8, 110, 121
actor-network theory 15, 33, 40, 92–3; *see also* translation
Akrich, M. 15
algorithms 52, 61–2, 66–71, 77
Allais, M. 68
Anteby, M. 102
Arizona Stock Exchange 61, 63, 67, 69
Austin, J.L. 8–9, 14, 18
Ayache, E. 19

Barings Bank 59
Baudrillard, J. 20–1, 81
Beck, J. 13
Beckett, S. 66–7
Bergson, H. 70
Bezes, P. 115
Bichler, S. 105
Black, F. 68
Boltanski, L. 9
Burroughs, W. 13
business education 96–7, 103; case method in 97–102; finance in 103–6
business schools *see* business education

Cage, J. 13
Callon, M. 9–10, 15, 38, 92–3, 120
capital *see* capitalization
capitalization 29, 40, 97, 103–7, 120, 122, 125
Cartwright, N. 38
Centre National d'Études Spatiales 111
Chiapello, È. 9
Christensen, C.R. 101–2
Collège de France 29, 35, 97
Colloque de Cerisy 35–6
Computer Assited Trading System 68
Cooren, F. 13–15
Coriat, B. 9

Cotation Assistée en Continu 68
cybernetics 73–4
Czarniawska, B. 14

Deleuze, G. 19, 21, 29–30, 97, 99, 114, 123
Derrida, J. 19
Descola, P. 35–6
description 17–20, 113, 127–9; complexity of 52, 58–60; of financial objects 45–8, 50–4, 55, 57–8; and the state 109–11, 113–14, 118
Despret, V. 88
Desrosières, A. 118–9
Dewey, J. 14, 16, 40, 102
Dior 84
Doganova, L. 33
Donham, W.B. 100
Dumont, L. 30
Dupuy, J.-P. 64, 73–4

École des Mines de Paris 11, 125
École Polytechnique 111
economic anthropology 33–34
economics 30–2; 37–8; 62, 66, 68, 73, 89, 100, 114; experiments in 63, 89–91; *see also* economization
economization 38–9, 113–8
embeddedness 64–5, 72, 74–6
Epictetus 97
Europe 13, 114, 125–6
European Research Council 125
experimentation 23, 87–88, 91–4; participant observation in 89–91; in economics 63, 89–91; *see also* testing
explicitness 24–6, 70, 127–9; and equilibrium 64–9; of financial objects 52; and the state 109–10, 113–4, 117–19, 121, 123–5
Eyquem-Renault, M. 33

financial exchange 22, 47, 75–6, 62; automation of 61–3, 67-70
financial products 19–20, 53–4, 77–78
Fisher, I. 106–7
focus groups 31, 80–1
Foerster, H. von 73–4
Foucault, M. 21, 29–30, 97, 99, 114, 123
Fraser, C.E. 101
French Ministry of Higher Education and Research 109, 111, 115–17, 119–21, 124
Freud, S. 22
Friedman, D. 63
Funt, A. 24

Gaglio, G. 32, 80–1
Garcia, M.-F. 65
Garfinkel, H. 13
Godelier, M. 33–4
Goffman, E. 12
Grandclément, C. 32, 80–1
Granovetter, M. 65
Greimas, A. J. 14
Gropius, W. 72
Guala, F. 66
Guyer, J. 34

Habermas, J. 114
Hacking, I. 35
Harvard Business School 96–7, 99–103, 106
Harvard Law School 100
Heidegger, M. 23
Heraclitus 101
Hertz, E. 22

Ibáñez, J. 73
Illich, I. 74
International Swaps and Derivatives Association 53
investment banking 46–8, 55–8, 122; back office in 48–50, 52–4, 58–60; information systems in 50–2, 58–60
Izquierdo, A.J. 24, 30

James, W. 16, 101

Kaplan, S. 33
Kaprow, A. 13
Kerviel, J. 59
Klossowski, P. 21
Knuth, D. 66

Langdell, C.C. 100
Latour, B. 11, 15, 18, 23, 26, 33, 36, 88
Law, J. 15, 18
Lazarsfeld, P. 13
Le Corbusier 72
Leeson, N. 59
Leibniz, G. W. 64
Lépinay, V.-A. 45–6
Lévi-Strauss, C. 21
Lewin, K. 13
Lezaun, J. 31, 80
Linhardt, D. 115
liquidity 46, 62–3, 67, 71, 78
Loi Organique Relative aux Lois de Finances 109–10, 112–21, 123
Luhmann, N. 73
Lyotard, J.-F. 8–10, 110

MacKenzie, D. 10, 30, 92, 103–4
management 8–10, 32–33, 113–18; see also management consulting
management consulting 1, 22, 32–33, 109, 123
Marcus Aurelius 97
marketing 32, 79–89
Marx, K. 29
Maurer, B. 34
Mead, G.H. 14
measure see performance measurement
Merton, R.K. 13
Milgram, S. 13, 24
Millo, Y. 30
Mirowski, P. 67
Mitchell, T. 31
Mol, A. 48
Moreno, J.L. 13
Morris, C.W. 14

naturalism 35–8, 61–2, 80–1, 86–8
Naville, P. 9
neoliberalism 30–1, 108, 113–15, 119–20
New York Stock Exchange 63, 68, 75, 78
Nietzsche, F. 21
Nitzan, J. 105

Ogien, A. 113
Organisation for Economic Co-operation and Development 119, 121

Paris Bourse 61, 63–4, 67–9, 75, 77–8
Pask, G. 73
Peirce, C.S. 14, 16, 101

performance measurement 86–8, 108–10, 118–21, 123
performativity: performative turn 2–4, 7, 15–17, 26, 28, 35, 127–8; and business 32–3, 96, 103, 105; and critique 128–30; as dramaturgical accomplishment 11–3, 81; and economics 29–31, 34, 38, 62; as efficacy 8–10, 110; and finance 19, 55, 58, 75; and marketing 32, 78–82, 89-91; of measurement 86–8, 108–10, 123; and naturalism 35–8, 61–2; 86–8; in organizational semiotics 13–15, 32–3, 92, 108; performative utterances 17–18; in science studies 10–1, 23, 30–1, 36, 80, 87–8; *see also* performance measurement
perfume 82–91
Pickering, A. 10
Pinch, T. 92
Polanyi, K. 29, 65
pragmatism 2–3, 7, 14–19, 21–3, 38, 40, 46, 69, 96, 100–2
Preda, A. 75
prices 61, 64, 67, 69–71, 76, 78; *see also* valuation; *see also* financial exchange; *see also* liquidity
provocation 23–4, 113, 28; and market research 79–82; *see also* experimentation
psychoanalysis 21–2, 49, 97
public finance 113–18

Quattrone, P. 33, 39

realization 12, 21–2, 89–90, 98, 107, 113, 125–6, 128–30
Reich, W. 13
Rousseau, J.J. 19
Rowe, C. 72
Royce, J. 101
Rust, J. 63

Sartre, J.-P. 12
Schmitt, C. 114
science and technology policy 115–16, 119–23, 125–6
Searle, J. 8, 14
Seneca 97
Serres, M. 92
Sims, B. 92
simulacrum 20–2, 70–1, 81–4, 91, 97, 99, 103, 107, 113, 127–9
Sloterdijk, P. 26
Slutsky, R. 72
Smith, V. 63
social studies of finance 30, 55–8; 61
Société Générale 59
Spinoza, B. 21
state: theory of the 108–10, 113–15, 122, 125–6
statistics *see* performance measurement

Taylor, J.R. 13
testing: consumer tests 1–2, 82–89, 93–5; sociology of 91–3
Thévenot, L. 66
Toronto Stock Exchange 68
translation 22, 92–5, 121
transparency 59, 62, 65, 72–5, 116

valuation 1, 40, 55–8, 97, 104–7; *see also* capitalization
Van Every, E.J. 13
Varela, F. 73
Vatin, F. 9
virtual 20, 26, 69–71, 95

Walras, L. 62, 64, 68, 70
Warhol, A. 13
Weber, M. 29
Weick, K. 14
Wunsch, S. 63

Zelizer, V. 34